How To Get Out Of Work

How To Get Out Of Work

"A Framework for Manipulation, Deception, and Misdirection."

Alexander
Oakes

Cover Design: Michael Spano
Interior Design: Creative Publishing Book Design

This book is dedicated to my brother, Zach.
Life or death, brothers forever.

Table of Contents

What is Motivation

*We are all ingrained with evil to one degree or another. Fair enough. But what is evil? We feel, smell, taste, hear, and even see its aftermath, but we are unable to see IT. We know it intimately yet we cannot quantify it with numerical certainty. Perhaps evil and good do not exist in the binary we know them. That is, as separate, identifiable factions pitted against one another in eternal opposition; rather, perhaps they engage in a symbiotic balance that creates the conditions necessary for a fulfilled human experience. For one cannot exist without the other. Therefore, if good cannot exist without evil as an antithesis, what is good but reliant on evil? Is good, in fact, evil? Are they perhaps kinsmen? A tsunami and a cliff wherein one without the other is useless and unable to show its force and power? Furthermore, how are we as humans to decipher evil from good when no clear line could ever be logically drawn across the entirety of the shared human experience? —**Alexander Oakes***

"That person is bad." Have you ever heard someone say this phrase? Chances are you have, or at least words similar to this and, if so, you probably either agreed with the person speaking, or disagreed and instead chose to defend this allegedly bad person. Think back to that moment, if you can, and think about which response was correct in hindsight. Was the person good or were they bad? Do you have an answer? Well what if I told you that my belief is that technically there are no *good* or *bad* people?

If this statement sounds absurd, the idea that good and bad people do not exist that is, I implore you to ask yourself what the words good and bad actually mean when it comes to human behavior, because I would wager that your idea of good and bad differs significantly from vast swaths of the world population, and that is only speaking in terms of the current population. This is to say that if we were to go through all of the annals of human history seeking out the ethical elements that have made up the moral foundations of each and every subculture to ever exist, well, I imagine there would be a fair amount for us here in the 21st century to argue about. In other words, when it comes to this issue who are you to presume that your version of *good*, if any, is right? I mean, if 85% of the world gets their morals from religion and there are 4,000-10,000 religions being practiced globally right now (all of which still influence non-religious people mind you), statistically you should just assume you have it wrong regardless of what you believe. I digress though.

You see, each and every political and/or religious ideology, a distinction becoming ever more muddied in our modern world I might add, and even the subsets of those ideologies have their own specific sets of parameters when it comes to good and bad (i.e., Christianity could be subdivided into Protestant and Catholic, and then those ideologies could be further subdivided into specific doctrines, etc.). In other words, a Catholic will enjoy a cold beer with their dinner after they give thanks to their Judeo-Christian interpretation of God while a Southern Baptist praying to that same God before their meal couldn't even begin to imagine engaging in such sinful behavior.

A hardline Democrat will vote for an increase in welfare spending because they want to help underprivileged individuals while a hardline Conservative will vote against this spending because they believe that welfare incentivizes self-destructive behavior and ultimately hurts underprivileged communities. And a spiritual hippie, behind his wife's back, drops acid and shags some stranger in his van while across the world a traditional Muslim, smoking hashish to ease his hunger pains during Ramadan, stones his adulterous wife in order to cleanse her soul via the Hudud punishment called Rajm. Get the picture? In essence, regardless of how stark the differences are between these examples, at the end of the day all of these people performing all of these acts are doing what they deem to be *good*. But who is right?

SIDENOTE

Even though, as you will see, I am not a huge believer in objective right and/or objective wrong, at least not in terms of human behavior that is, in this book I do still use the words good and bad quite often. Therefore, it is important here at the outset that I clarify what I mean when I say these words. Essentially, my definition of these words is based on the moral standards of acceptable behavior (Overton Window) in whatever society and/or subculture I am referencing at the time. I.e., for you and me here in modern day America it may be *good* that first-degree pre-meditated murder is illegal, regardless of the context. However, in a culture where avenging a loved one is not only legal, but also encouraged, this may not be the case. Ergo, in a technical sense whether murder is a good or bad behavior depends almost entirely on the context of your environment. Make sense?

Answering this question, "who is right," is actually rather difficult. Hell, it may even be impossible because, in my summation, what is right and wrong appears to be subjective. With that said, though, I still think that it is a worthwhile query because my journey to answer questions like these actually ended up being a foundational part of research, and then years later this book. This is to say that, as I began to write this book, I found myself focusing quite a bit on morality, mainly because, at the time, I wanted to establish what the base incentive was behind every action we engage in, every word we speak, and every sentence we write, and, to me, morality seemed like a good place to start. Well, as fate would have it this interest in morality subsequently led to me having to ask questions like, why should I care about right or wrong in the first place? And furthermore, why do some people intentionally choose paths that society deems wrong while others go the route of purity and goodness?

Now, full disclosure, these aspects of human behavior and decision-making are still fascinating to me, however, answering the questions that these questions led me to were even more intriguing, and they were also where this book truly began to take shape. At any rate, this second line of questioning, which consisted of questions like *what is going on when we communicate with one another, what are the underlying motivations and actual desired outcomes of our communications,* and also *what leads to success or failure among these manipulative dances that humans have come to know as communications* eventually became a quantitative and qualitative longitudinal study of communication that used interviews, cross-sectional survey data, and observational research methods to test several hypotheses. The resulting findings of this aforementioned methodology led me first to a research thesis, and then to the thesis of this book, which is as follows:

> **Thesis:** *Every single action conducted by human beings, and in particular our communications, are not inherently good or bad, but rather self-serving. Therefore, all communication is, to some degree or another, a strategic manipulation designed to achieve some self-serving purpose. With this in mind, it is the thesis of this work that all false communications, henceforth known as lies, can be described as existing in four dimensions, and lies that fall within the first and third dimensions can be used to manipulate with far greater efficiency and/or success than those that fall within the second and fourth dimensions. Furthermore, this dimensional system of false stories can be used in concert with a novel system of personality archetype classification to manipulate and/or control interpersonal communications with expertise and precision, in any scenario.*

Alright, so now you know the thesis of this book. Before going any further, though, I do need to pause for a moment and just quickly state that, despite the obvious ethical concerns associated with this work, it should be known that the purpose of such work is that individuals can achieve and maintain a higher level of control and power over their own life, which is already being influenced by the constant pushing and pulling of everyone else's personal agendas and/or self-serving objectives. In other words, it is my belief that this pushing and pulling is an inherent reality of humanity's communication landscape, and therefore, this work simply strives to help people better understand and/or manipulate the debatably grim moral reality in which they already exist. A reality that will, in fact, be manipulated for them by others if they choose to ignore it and simply sit idly by in optimistic bliss. Ergo, even though this thesis sounds rather dark, it is actually designed to help people live a more fulfilled life that they, and they alone control. Make sense? Great, then let's move on.

Ok, even though you now have a rough idea of where I am starting from, there is still a fair bit more we need to discuss before we get into the nitty-gritty of how to actually use communication to manipulate others. To begin, what do I mean by self-serving? I mean, sure, I imagine you know the obvious answers, and at this very moment I would even bet that things like chasing money, trying to get laid, and putting money in the offering plate only when everyone is looking are coming to mind, yeah? Well, yes, those actions are indeed self-serving, but in this book, I want to go farther than that by also convincing you that even good actions are self-serving. Let me explain.

Take, for instance, communication. Ask yourself this, what is communication? I mean, we have been taught that communication serves the functions of bringing us closer together, encouraging cooperative behavior, separating us from the animals, and allowing us to live a more fulfilled human experience. I.e., you shoot the shit, smoke the breeze, and make friends. Believe me, I am a major fan and communication seems like not only a great gift, but also one that we can use to improve humanity, does it not? Of course, with that said, when you use communication, even for *good* reasons, at the deepest and most base level, you aren't *really* being good at all, are you? To explain, let's look at some examples.

When you go to work, a fundamental aspect of modern life, you are likely doing it to make money so that you can maintain a certain quality of life, either for yourself or others; or perhaps you just like staying busy and need purpose. When you eat, a fundamentally unavoidable aspect of life, you are hoping to maintain your health and stave off hunger pains by ingesting nutrition and calories. When you drink alcohol and/or self-medicate with drugs you are numbing the things that take away from your joy and fulfillment by enjoying the release of endorphins and hormones that the alcohol and drugs artificially produce. All of these things are beneficial to you in some way or another, agreed? No? Are you still on the fence about these being self-serving, or do you think that these are, yes, partially self-serving, but the real reason you do them is for others? I.e., perhaps you say, "Well at my job I help people," or maybe you think that you eat so that you can remain alive to take care of your kids. Furthermore, maybe the drugs, alcohol, or whatever your crutch is helps you to be a better member of society by suppressing your *bad* side. Fair enough, but let's go a little deeper.

SIDENOTE

By social standing I mean, in essence, how the social environment you value evaluates you. For example, a high social standing looks very different for a "made" man in the mafia than it does for a financial analyst in that each of these two people will have their own, very different set of hurdles to jump if they want to be seen as valuable by their peers. I.e., each of these two people are in different social groups with drastically different standards of *good*.

Put plainly, you are always the primary benefactor of your good actions, even when you are doing things that seem like they are selfless. This is to say that seemingly generous actions still benefit you significantly in two distinct ways, and the first of these is by giving you that desirable feeling of being "good." Now I know that sounds a bit silly, but the reality is that this feeling is actually much more than just some abstract sensation that comes out of nowhere. In fact, this occurrence, doing good things because they make us feel better, is known as the empathy-joy hypothesis and it is rooted in our very evolution. Anyway, don't worry, we will get more into this concept in a minute.

Now the second way that being good provides a benefit to you is by increasing your social standing in whatever social groups/subcultures you are a part of, and these social groups/subcultures, mind you, could range all the way from the entire planet, say if you were a world leader of a major country operating within an international organization, to, for instance, a musician trying to impress the fan base of a local indie rock scene. Hell, these social groups/subcultures could even go all the way down to a family unit consisting of only a few people, even though this is not what we normally think about when we think about social environments.

At any rate, the reason that this second type of benefit from good behavior exists is because good behavior, whatever that is for the group, leads to better evaluations/judgments from that group, which ultimately leads to a higher social standing within that environment. In other words, you may think that you are a lone wolf, independent, or that you just don't care about your social standing, but this is more than a popularity contest I am talking about here. So stay with me.

You see, high social standing has been seen as good in every single social environment ever established, and this elevated social standing also often leads to social rewards such as gaining people's trust, becoming more hirable, and better selection of a mate. And this is because every society/subculture ever established, without exception, has preferred that people follow its version of good behavior, whatever that may be, to its version of bad behavior. Ergo, even though you may think that you are just "doing your own thing" when you engage in good behavior, the truth is that there is a 50/50 chance that you are using this second way of benefiting from good deeds and trying to meet some sort of societal standard for yourself, even if that is just maintaining a social standing that keeps you out of prison; or depending on where you live and whom you hang out with, gets you into prison (Looking at you drill rappers). Anyway, our understanding of this second benefit of good behavior can be enhanced by taking a look at and understanding the empathy-altruism hypothesis and the wary cooperation theory, which I will delve into after I, as promised, discuss the empathy-joy hypothesis.

So, to begin, the empathy-joy hypothesis, which was established by Kyle Smith, Jack Keating, and Ezra Stotland, in essence states that "people feeling empathic concern help to get the pleasure of sharing vicariously in the joy that the target of empathy feels when his or her need is removed." In other words, this hypothesis suggests that when we help others it is because, when we do, we actually get to experience the same positive emotions that we would have experienced if we had received the assistance ourselves. I.e., we get to experience the feeling of getting help vicariously. Make sense?

SIDENOTE

You may be wondering, "what about psychopaths or people who do good things begrudgingly because they dislike the person they are helping?" First off, psychopaths make up less than 5% of the population, so they are an anomaly, but as far as the people doing good things "because it is simply what's right," stay tuned, we will get there.

Ok, going beyond the observational and theoretical work of Smith, Keating, and Stotland, in 2013 Japanese researchers by the names of Hiroaki Kawamichi, Hiroki Tanabe, Haruka Takahashi, and Norihiro Sadato sought to use functional magnetic resonance imaging (fMRI) to further study the empathy-joy hypothesis, and to do this they created a virtual ball toss game within a digital environment wherein some of the participants were isolated without a ball and some were able to roam freely. Now the purpose of this experiment, in which the participants who did have the ball could choose to either throw the ball to the isolated player or continue to exclude them from the game, was, essentially, to see how the participants reacted to each other when they were not being directed. Well, put plainly, what these researchers found was nothing short of fascinating, at least from the perspective of someone studying the empathy-joy hypothesis, that is.

When it was all said and done and the experiment had concluded, the resulting data showed that over half of the participants with balls chose to share. Furthermore, out of these participants who chose to share (again, they were all being monitored via fMRI the entire time), a staggering 100% of them experienced activation of the bilateral dorsal striatum, AKA the part of the brain that is associated with positive feelings/emotions. In other words, this data showed the researchers, and then the world, that the players did not just *say* they were feeling better after assisting the isolated players, which could have happened if they had perceived social pressure from the people running the study, but rather that their brains truly *did* experience these changes. Ergo, this study quantitatively demonstrated, for the first time, the scientific validity of the idea that we do good things, in part, because it feels good and/or because our brains actually reward us for it on the back end. Fascinating, right?

Ok, moving on, as I mentioned earlier there is also a second reason why we do good things, although I do have to say that, at first, this one seems a bit like a contradiction. In other words, stay with me. Anyway, this second type of benefit is the increase in social standing people get from doing good things, and it can be explained by looking at the empathy-altruism hypothesis and the wary cooperation theory.

Beginning with the former of those two aforementioned concepts, according to Dr. Charles Daniel Batson the empathy-altruism hypothesis posits that "empathic concern (an other-oriented emotional response elicited by and congruent with the perceived welfare of someone in need) produces altruistic motivation (a motivational state with the ultimate goal of reducing that need)." In other words, this statement by Dr. Batson, and the empathy-altruism hypothesis as a whole, believes that humans help one another because when we see a person in distress we actually end up feeling empathy towards them, which then leads to a desire to remedy their situation, and unlike the empathy-joy hypothesis, according to this school of thought these "selfless" actions are not motivated by internal feelings of joy, but rather by an outward-facing need to help others, even when there is no perceived gain associated with helping.

SIDENOTE

Now if you are like me, at face value this trait doesn't really seem all that much like one that was developed evolutionarily, does it? Rather, it seems more like something that makes humans special, right? Well, this is actually wrong. I.e., if right now you are thinking that this empathy-altruism hypothesis contradicts my opinion that everything we do is self-serving, I suppose that, in a vacuum, you would be right. But don't get too excited, though, because there is still another aspect of this second benefit that will make things a bit clearer.

Alright, so moving ever onward, it is important to understand that in the empathy-altruism model peoples' altruistic motivations are not always explicit. What I mean by this is that, in essence, the individual helping is not always consciously aware of what they can get out of the situation. However, even with that said this does not mean that these "selfless" actors are still not aware of the potential benefits somewhere deep down in their subconscious minds. To explain, let's look at a theory called wary cooperation that, when combined with the empathy-altruism hypothesis helps explain how empathetic/altruistic behavior is still just an evolutionarily developed, and personally beneficial trait.

Now, what is wary cooperation and how does it fit into this puzzle? Well, in essence this theory, which was developed by two men named John Alford and John Hibbing in 2004 (*The Origin of Politics: An Evolutionary Theory of Political Behavior*) posits that "Humans are cooperative, but not altruistic; competitive, but not exclusively so. We have an innate inclination to cooperate, particularly within defined group boundaries, but we are also highly sensitive to selfish actions on the part of other group members. This sensitivity leads us to cease cooperating when that cooperation is not reciprocated, to avoid future interaction with non-cooperators, and even to engage in personally costly punishment of individuals who fail to cooperate."

In lay terms, this statement denies, or rather redefines outright altruism and instead explains it as being a natural evolution of human behavior that is used as a means of improving one's social standing, and subsequently their overall quality of life, by giving people the ability to resonate (feel empathy toward) with others, which allows those people to work with others whom they are not related to. To put that another way, imagine being all by yourself without any of our modern luxuries in a world of raiding tribes and saber tooth tigers. In that world, can you see how it might be evolutionarily beneficial to find ways of getting along with a group (because, again, humans survive best in groups)? Furthermore, can you also see how evolving to feel empathy would help you with this and how that could also condition you to feel positive when you engage in altruistic behavior? I.e., isn't it entirely possible that, as a species, we simply developed empathy so that we would be driven to help others because, even if there is no *immediate* benefit when it comes to helping these others, overall this altruistic trait will still increase our chances of getting into an in-group?

Anyway, the key takeaway from all three of these theories is that, as much of a bummer as it is to hear, empathy, selflessness, and kindness are just evolutionarily beneficial developed traits, not something divine that makes us special. In other words, these traits lead to altruistic/

selfless behavior, and then that behavior leads to positive feelings when cooperating with others, which is evolutionarily beneficial to us, not only because it feels good, but also because it actually increases our gene's chances of survival by allowing us to be a part of a group, thus giving us the strength of numbers. Got it?

Ok, so at this point you may still not be completely off the fence about the self-serving motivations underlying everything we do, including the good things, and to be honest, that's ok. I mean, I recognize that it is a big and bitter pill to swallow. But with that said, you do have to admit that, given everything we have just talked about, it would be pretty hard to argue that everything we do isn't at least in *some* way tied to our evolutionary development and/or our built-in biological rewards system. At any rate, though, for those of you who are still having trouble accepting all of this, just know that this information doesn't necessarily have to be bad news because this reality is not in and of itself a net negative in regard to the flourishing of humanity. I.e., you buy a homeless person lunch, watch your kids open Christmas presents, pray, fuck, and fight the bad guy who smacked your ole lady's ass at the bar; sure, all of these actions gave you something in return, but that's nothing to be ashamed of. You see, being self-serving is as inherent to human beings as it is to any other living creature and you are in no way guilty of choosing to possess this biological drive any more than you are guilty of choosing to not want to die and/or experience pain. In other words, it is simply our nature to do things that benefit us and avoid things that don't. Ergo, whether you are a crooked Wall Street stockbroker working for your third beach house or a devout nun slaving away until she gets her heavenly payday, in the end we are all the same when it comes to who we really serve, ourselves.

So moving on, at this point you may be wondering why we are talking about our self-serving nature when this is technically supposed to be a book about how to get out of work? Well, I suppose the reason for this is because, as I suggested earlier, this realization about our behavior is actually what got all of this started in the first place, and therefore, is also an important part of the foundation of my research. This is to say that after I developed my theory on why we do what we do, I then began to ask questions about the communication process in particular. And in doing so I quickly began to realize that this self-serving nature did, in fact, apply to that aspect of our behavior as well, especially when it came to deception. In other words, up until making this discovery communication, and specifically deceptive communication, had seemed very abstract and ambiguous to me because it just didn't make sense how the same lie told in two different environments could have drastically different outcomes. However, after I began to understand the motivations of each party involved in these deceptive dances, this confusing portrait started to come into focus. Ergo, what I had not been taking into account was that in each of these scenarios what had actually been different was not the lie, per say, but rather how that lie factored into the personal objectives of the person receiving that lie. Anyway, we will get more into this, and also how to craft a lie for each type of person later, but for right now I just needed you to know that this discussion about our underlying motivation is not some random rabbit hole. Instead, it is a very important part of the manipulation process that you will need to, at some point, accept.

SIDENOTE

Manipulation is a very scary word in our culture. It spurs on thoughts of seedy back-alley con men and emotionally abusive significant others. With that said, though, moving forward throughout the rest of this book, with the exception of the parts that specifically involve deception of course, understand that when I say manipulation I am simply referring to an individual doing and/or saying something in order to alter another individual's thoughts and/or subsequent behavior. Ergo, manipulation can be as tame and friendly as telling a physically unattractive person they look nice as a way of making them feel better, or as sinister as convincing your significant other that you are not *really* cheating on them, even when you are. In other words, manipulation does not always connotate something "bad," and therefore, when you hear manipulation do not fret until you know the context of the situation.

Alright, if you have made it this far, I have good news. It is finally time to talk about communication. To begin, when human beings communicate with individuals and/or groups, we are constantly attempting to manipulate/alter the thought processes and by proxy the actions of the other party through that communication, verbal or non-verbal, and this manipulative dance is taking place whether we realize it or not. I.e., every flutter of the eyes, change in speech cadence, and gesture of body language is continually being analyzed by both parties, and this applies even to the simplest of communications. For example, if I ask my wife to hand me a bottle of water, I am attempting to convince her to stop what she is doing in order to expend calories moving her body for a purpose that benefits me; and since this request is a small and routine ask, when I say it normally her body reads my voice/body language, clears it as ok, and then she says "yes" and does it. I then see her casually grabbing the bottle and smiling as she hands it to me. Ergo, in return, my subconscious clears her voice/body language and because everything checks out, I take it and drink.

In this scenario, as silly as it seems because it is so simple, in a technical sense I used my verbal and non-verbal communication to manipulate my wife into getting a bottle of water. Conversely, her reply of "yes," followed by her friendly body language and normal facial expressions manipulated me to take it and trust that it was safe to drink, and the end result is that I benefit from ingesting water and she benefits by "feeling good about herself for helping" and/or by fortifying our mutually beneficial pair-bond relationship (marriage). Make sense? Well what if instead I had screamed my request for water while spinning in circles? I mean, in that scenario surely her subconscious would register some red flags and her first move would not be to grab me water, agreed? Even stranger, imagine that I had asked sinisterly and placed a pause in between the words "me", and "a bottle of water" while also saying the second part in a seemingly over-the-top ominous tone. Would she get it for me then; or, again, would she look at me and register that something was off?

Now I am not a betting man, but if I was, I would wager that she would go with the second option, and the reason for this is that when I behaved in this strange manner, in an instant her subconscious would ask itself if I had a pattern of sinister behavior, no, and if there had been any other changes to my behavior lately, also no. Then, after a few seconds more, her subconscious would have asked hundreds if not thousands of other questions aimed at figuring out why this seems like more than a normal quotidian ask and came to the conclusion that something was not right. Ergo, even though my objective was the same in these latter scenarios, my execution was not, and as a result my manipulation failed; all because of my wife's subconscious analysis of my communication.

SIDENOTE

The reason that this is important is because you should not for a second think that even the dullest people among us, intellectually speaking, are not watching you and making constant mental evaluations of both your relevant and irrelevant behaviors. You see, to the primal competitive beast that is our nature, quite literally everything around us could be useful information because our cognition simply does not know exactly what we will need to use later on down the line, and this applies to all humans, mind you, not just the intelligent ones. Case in point, during my field research I actually found myself in more than a few embarrassing situations simply because I had underestimated the subconscious minds of several individuals who seemed to be otherwise blissfully unaware of their surroundings. Well, put plainly this mistake of underestimation is not one I make anymore because I now understand that human beings, yes, even the dullards, are incredible processing machines when it comes to naturally understanding patterns of human behavior, as well as deviations in those patterns. Ergo, keep this information about how we analyze communication in the back of your mind now so that you do not have to learn these lessons, as I did, the hard way.

Anyway, that's enough of a rabbit hole about my fictitious wife. To get us back on track, in sum, even communication itself is self-serving in that it is, essentially, just another form of manipulation designed to help us use others to reach our desired goals. With that in mind, if you are going to take control of your environment, something that I hope you will be more proficient at by the end of this book, it is crucial that you, like I did, come to understand and accept this foundational element of our human nature. And in addition to this, you should also come to understand/accept that there is no such thing as purposeless communication, only inconsequential communication because everything we do, technically speaking, is a byproduct of our self-serving nature, even if it seems irrelevant (I.e., giving a compliment to a stranger actually has a self-serving purpose, even though it doesn't seem like it.). Furthermore, if you are to use this book with success, remember that you are constantly under observation by those around you and that their evaluations of you *will* impact how they see you, and subsequently, how they communicate with you, which is something that will become extremely important when we get into how to actually control the manipulative communication dances you engage in during your day-to-day life. All good? Great. Then let's move on.

Alright folks, it has taken me a little while to get here, but before I told you why I wrote this book I needed you to understand a few foundational elements of my worldview because, well, otherwise a lot of this book wouldn't make sense. At any rate, now that you do, I want to get into this book's purpose. In essence, despite the provocative title of this work my goal in these pages isn't some hacky attempt to give you all of the secrets to lying. Rather, it is simply a framework that you can use as a tool to help you establish more control over your own life and/or be more aware of your surroundings. In other words, the goal of this book is simply to help your success rate when it comes to communicative interactions by explaining the inner working of the manipulation/communication process and also by condensing/distilling all of my research into a usable system of classifying lies and how people change with power.

Now, as to how I actually went about doing this, as my thesis stated, I have developed four categories in which all lies can fit; and in addition to this, I have also attempted to create six archetypes that broadly represent and describe the ways in which people change with real and/or perceived power, which will become important later on in the book because, as it turns out, individuals are far easier to manipulate when you can give them the perception of power over you. Anyway, when used together these two aspects of my research, in conjunction with a thorough understanding of the other elements of the manipulation process, allow anyone with an in depth under-standing of these principles to take control of the dances we engage in every time we communicate with others. Ergo, these two aspects, along with a few foundational theories/concepts that make them more understandable, are what I outline in this book and what you will use to take that aforementioned control. Got it?

SIDENOTE

I laugh when people read self-help books promising *the* secret technique(s) needed to find success. Perhaps you will find some substance in those books, but in my experience something that seems too good to be true generally is. So, with that said, despite the fact that it technically sounds better to say that I will "give you the secret formula," in reality no such formula exists. This is to say that humans and/or social environments are extremely complex, and therefore, if I was to give you specific "hard" rules, in the end you would be rather limited. Ergo, in my view a broad framework works much better because this framework, which contains the principles and concepts needed to manipulate others, can be used effectively in any scenario. I.e., I am teaching you about how vehicles work in general, not simply teaching you how to fix a few specific makes and models. Make sense?

Ok, so before closing out this chapter, I would be remiss if I didn't remind you one last time, for those concerned with the ethics of this work anyway, that this is not just a book for bullshitters. This is to say that it is also a book for people who find themselves being duped and taken to the proverbial woodshed on a regular basis by more proficient communicators. Case in point, my close friend, and one of my motivations to study this topic, has always had issues with interpersonal communications. I.e., whether they were getting roped into buying a timeshare, losing authority over their employees at work, or just being suckered into staying with a cheating significant other for far too long, this individual's life was a mess because this person was a passive participant in their own existence just floating down the river of life and seeing what direction the current took them. Well, more accurately, seeing what direction other people in the river pulled them. At any rate, after working with this friend, no, they didn't all of a sudden become a slick car salesman making "bank" on commission. Nor did they begin bedding women way out of their league. What they did do, however, was take over the reins of their communicative interactions with other people. And the result of this change was that they quit getting duped, pushed around, and cheated on. Put another way, by learning the framework outlined in this book they learned to spot red flags, have a good defense with a better offense, and just in general to stop being naïve about how much of the world around us is just perceived reality, not objective reality (Objective and Perceived reality are concepts I discuss in the next chapter). Ergo, yes, this book does teach people how to manipulate others, but this does not mean it is exclusively for shysters.

Alright, we are almost done folks so bear with me. Moving on, just so you can't say I didn't warn you, politics and religion will occasionally come up in this book. Now to what degree these parts annoy you will depend on how salient these issues are for you. I.e., if you are a political junkie, like me, or a religious fundamentalist, like many in my family, well, there may be some things that drive you up a wall within these pages. Hell, I have probably already done that in this chapter alone. With that said, though, despite the fact that I obviously have my own, very strong personal views on these topics, my goal in the following pages is not to convert people. In other words, I don't care what religion, if any, you are, and I don't care whether you are an Anarcholibertarian or the world's most outspoken socialist. What I do care about, however, is that people learn to spot the ways in which we manipulate one another, and also to learn to do it themselves. At any rate, since religion and politics have mastered these things for thousands of years and are therefore great examples of how the manipulation process works in real life, I might use them, should the occasion call for it.

Ok, final thing and then we are done. When it comes to my qualifications for writing this book, in sum, during my 28 years on this planet my credits include starting a very successful business that made tens of thousands of dollars selling drugs, booze, and jailbroken iPod touches to fellow teenagers in my southern county at age 14, running a fake ID business out of the barracks during my time in the Marine Corps, and coming back alive from multiple combat deployments while working as a machine gunner (0331) and also as part of a human intelligence team. Furthermore, I have also gained a master's degree in political psychology from Arizona State University (Summa Cum Laude), worked on various university-funded research projects focused on cognition/information processing, and most recently I have conducted a 4-year qualitative ethnographic study across multiple places of business to see what I can and can't get away with if I have the right story, as well as a year's worth of collecting quantitative cross-sectional data regarding the 4 dimensions of lying. In other words, I am a dirtbag, and a damn good one at that. But I am also, however, someone who has stumbled into the social sciences research section of academia and someone who believes that I have just a weird enough view of the world that I can help bring some of that research to everyday people in an easy-to-understand, and sometimes slightly fun way. Ergo, in a technical sense I may or may not be qualified to do this, but nonetheless I have.

Alright, with all of that said, I bid you farewell and hope you stick around to either call me a genius or a lunatic. Either way, I am moving on to the next chapter wherein I will be discussing what is real, a

What is Reality

Wise men speak because they have something to say;
Fools speak because they "have" to say something —**Plato**

Ok, so now that we have a foundation for why we do what we do, or at least this book's position on it, in this chapter we are going to move on to another foundational element of my research. This element covers the foundations of reality, as well as how our minds actually have a major role to play when it comes to constructing the world around us. Good to go? Great. Then to begin, ask yourself what is real and what exists only in your mind.

Now, when it comes to this question, my journey to answer it, unsurprisingly, began in the realm of philosophical research, and a common starting point I found in this realm, at least in regard to what connotates reality, was trying to first figure out how we can gain reliable knowledge. In other words, when it comes to figuring out what is real, according to philosophers the first step to answering this question is actually figuring out how to gather accurate information in the first place. I.e., just like a mechanic uses a code reader and/or other tools to find the cause of an illuminated "check engine light" instead of just making an educated guess about what is wrong, philosophers also use tools, such as philosophy, theology, and epistemology, to figure out questions about life and existence. Make sense?

SIDENOTE

On a personal note, I am not a huge fan of philosophy (the study of the fundamental nature of knowledge, reality, and existence), theology (the study of the nature of God and religious belief), or epistemology (the theory of knowledge, especially with regard to its methods, validity, and scope; the investigation of what distinguishes justified belief from opinion). I mean, sure, I can one hundred percent see how these are useful and important areas of study, but for me, though, these topics are generally not definitive enough. I.e., call me a simpleton, but I typically follow the KISS method in life, which stands for Keep It Simple Stupid.

Now as to the specific tools that philosophers use to find accurate information, the ones that ended up being the most compelling to me, at least when it comes to establishing "what is real and what is not real" that is, also happened to be two of the most popular and most researched philosophical methods found in modern academic literature. This is to say that during my research I was especially influenced by the rationalist school of thought, and the school of thought known as British empiricism. Now we won't be getting too deep into epistemological and metaphysical philosophy in this book (thank goodness), but I still want to cover these two concepts, albeit briefly, because, as I did in the first chapter, I want to take you on the same road that I traveled during my research in this one as well. Sound like a plan? Awesome, then let's get into it and establish what these two schools of thought actually are by looking into our not-so-distant past.

SIDENOTE

Empirical is defined by Webster's dictionary as "based on, concerned with, or verifiable by observation or experience rather than theory or pure logic."

Beginning with the former aforementioned concept, in the 17th century, a man by the name of Rene Descartes, who is commonly known as the father of modern philosophy, laid the foundation for what would later become rationalism. Essentially, what rationalism posits is that our reason, not empirical evidence gathered from our five senses, is the only surefire way to gather knowledge; and because of this, rationalists typically use a lot of complicated math, and/or deductive/inductive reasoning to find *true* answers. I.e., if I was, for instance, to ask a rationalist philosopher if their significant other was currently in their home, something that I think we can all agree is a rather basic question, they may not simply go look for their significant other in that home because, well, if they were to find their significant other in said home, how could they truly know that they were not hallucinating or seeing a body double? No, the five senses would simply not do for a rationalist, and therefore, instead of relying on their 5 senses to answer this query, they may instead begin by trying to find a way to establish that their significant other is specifically in their living room. And the reason for this is because this room is the one that their significant other frequents most often. Ergo, to this rationalist philosopher it is the most logical starting point.

At any rate, for this example let's assume that they do end up determining that their significant other is in the living room, be it by establishing that a light is on in the living room which indicates someone, most likely their significant other, is in there; or alternatively, maybe by doing some of their elaborate rationalist mind tricks (which I will not spend time on here). Either way, assuming that they do determine that their significant other is, in fact, most likely in the living room, then rationalists can use reason to deduce that their significant other is also, most likely, in the house. This is because the living room is in the house, and therefore, if their significant other is in the living room it is reasonable to assume that they are also in the house. Got it?

Now as you can see this type of thinking can make some things far more complicated than they need to be, at least in my opinion that is. I mean, Descartes himself, the godfather of this school of thought, once famously stated, as he sat and looked at a table in his home, that he could not truly know if he was looking at a table. So, yes, this school of thought can get a bit pedantic. However, to be fair to the rationalists, I will say that rationalism does get quite useful when talking about things we do not have empirical evidence of, such as making a reasonable argument for the existence of God or establishing a universally true and self-evident code of right vs wrong. But be that as it may, and despite how interesting it is, there is not nearly enough room here to talk about this side of rationalism. So for now just know that, put plainly, rationalism states that the only way to know what is and is not, is to trust your intellectual reason, not your lying eyes.

Ok, moving on to the second philosophical school of thought that informed my research for this chapter, standing in stark contrast

to the rationalists were the 18th-century British empiricists. Well, technically they were just empiricists, but because the main three proponents of this school of thought at the time, John Locke, George Berkely, and David Hume were from the British Isles, the name British empiricism stuck. At any rate, for parsimony let's just talk about one of these 18th-century British empiricists, David Hume.

In essence, Hume believed that the formation of any knowledge, or truth we could gain as a species would be derived from humanity's shared empirical experiences, which we get from our 5 senses, and not speculative concepts like reason and logic. In other words, if we all can see it, smell it, taste it, touch it, or hear it, then we can measure it and define it. Now as you can see this school of thought is very practical, thus why it is the foundation for things like the scientific method, but with that said, unfortunately, like Descartes and his table Hume also believed that experiences based upon our five senses are often susceptible to delusion. Therefore, even though he was still an empiricist, Humes' actual belief in regard to "how we know what we know" was that, at the end of the day, we can have no *true* knowledge at all, in the philosophical sense anyway, because there aren't any truly universal and/or shared human experiences. Ergo, in lay terms, according to Hume no one will experience one moment and/or thing in the exact same way, and because of this we cannot trust that our experiences are true based solely on our collective observations. Make sense?

Now I know that this school of thought, much like the rationalist school of thought, at face value seems a bit nonsensical and/or pompous when you realize that we have so many seemingly shared experiences, such as the sky being blue or that it hurts when we twist an ankle; but to get a little deeper, this theory, however pessimist, does logically track. The reason for this is because, and this is from Hume himself I might add, truth cannot be derived from our shared experiences, no matter how commonly agreed upon they may be, due to the fact that these "shared human experiences" are, in all reality, based primarily on the principle of correlation, which is commonly misinterpreted as causation, and are therefore not scientifically and/or logically sound. Let me explain.

SIDENOTE

Correlation is "a mutual relationship or connection between two or more things." Causation is "the relationship between cause and effect; causality."

Alright, don't worry, we are almost to the fun stuff, but just so you are staying with me on this journey, correlation, in essence, is the act of associating two things that commonly go together. I.e., to use one of the examples I found when first studying this term, if you believe that swans are white because that is the pattern you have seen in your everyday life, even if everyone else on the planet agrees that this is the case because they too have had this experience, in the end you are still just basing this belief on correlation. This is to say that, though going off of your own experiences makes it seem like swans are white, this is not causation and therefore is not a form of proof that would hold up in an academic study. To put that another way, in this particular "swan" case, you have simply noticed a pattern and formed a stereotype from it, the stereotype being that swans are white.

Now causation, on the other hand, which is what you would need if you were to actually prove that swans are white, would propose that

being a swan inherently causes you to be white because all swans are white. I.e., "that" dog is a mammal because all dogs are mammals. Ergo, regardless of your personal experiences (only seeing white swans throughout your life), you would not, in the above scenario, be able to accurately propose that all swans are white because there is such a thing as black swans, even though they are much harder to find in nature. Thus, your correlation about the color of swans is merely an inaccurate assumption, and therefore you cannot say it is *true* that all swans are white, even though white swans are all you, and pretty much everyone around you have ever seen.

SIDENOTE

At the risk of beating a dead horse, to give you another example of correlation; if you are trying to figure out if Republicans or Democrats smoke more you could do what is called a correlative study wherein you poll people about their political affiliations and smoking habits, with the goal being to observe the relationship. This is to say that, in order to find out if there is a relationship between partisanship and smoking you could collect data through questionnaires to help you see any patterns that may or may not exist. Now since this study has actually already been done (Gallup, 2004), let me skip to the end and let you know that there is, in fact, a relationship between these two variables and that on average 25% of Democrats smoke while only 21% of Republicans smoke. Pretty neat, right? Well, even though that aforementioned study does show a relationship between smoking and partisanship, nonetheless, from this study you could not surmise that simply being a Republican or a Democrat makes people smoke. And this is because causation requires the burden of data and proof. I.e., even if your correlative study was conducted perfectly with no mistakes, at the end of the day there could still be many alternative factors influencing why Democrats smoke more, all of which would need to be accounted for if you were to establish causation. In other words, perhaps Democrats are less religious and this is actually the reason they are represented more than Republicans in smoking statistics; or perhaps Democrats simply live in states where cigarettes are more accessible and therefore, they just have more access to smoking. At any rate, this is something called the third-variable problem, and also why it is so fucking hard to do a proper social science experiment that truly establishes causation.

Ok, that may have been a bit of an unnecessary tangent (though I would argue it is actually quite relevant to the manipulation process), but to bring this full circle to our little philosophy rabbit hole, in sum, from an empiricists perspective any shared human observation that is experienced through our five senses is never going to be completely accurate because everyone who has that experience will have it in a slightly different way; and as Hume points out in his writings, because of this anything we claim to know about the universe around us, whether it appears to be true or not, cannot be proven by our shared observations alone. Furthermore, these individual and/or shared observations, even if extremely similar to or even indistinguishable from one another, are open to largescale delusions because our five senses are often just plain inaccurate (If you think this to be false, look up the accuracy percentage of eyewitness testimony. I'll save you the trouble, it is in between 20 and 30 percent.) Ergo, given everything we have discussed in this chapter thus far, it appears to me that the main philosophical tools for finding knowledge, which we can then use to find true answers about the universe surrounding us, are either completely intangible (rationalism and reason) or, essentially, useless (empiricism and your lying eyes). Well, this is the conclusion that I reached anyway.

Continuing on, even though the answers I found in this quest were not quite as definitive as I had hoped, my time in the philosophical trenches wasn't a total wash, at least when it came to continuing my research that is. What I mean by this is that during this journey I discovered that, in essence, nobody knows what is real, and, frankly, I'm fine with that. This is to say that I don't actually need to know the ultimate truth of the universe because in my experience, and likely yours, this is not really needed to function and/or operate in daily life. In other words, from my perspective there is a universe that, it appears to me, has dependable laws and rules guiding it, regardless of if they are ultimately true or not, and we experience these rules every day when we interact with the world around us using the sensory organs that inform our five senses. I.e., place your hand on the stove after frying an egg, it feels hot, right? Well, one time of feeling this is good enough for me to know that the stove is always hot after cooking eggs, and furthermore, because I have talked to other people who have had this experience of interacting with a form of measurable and "real" reality, I know that I am not alone. Ergo, these things may not be ultimately true, but they certainly seem plainly obvious to any rational person that is alive today, whether they are a passionate follower of Descartes or have never studied philosophy a single day in their life. Anyway, this version of reality, a version governed by measurable laws and rules that we can all observe and agree upon, though not *ultimately* true, is one that I call **objective reality**, and it is what I want to discuss next.

SIDENOTE

As you will come to find out, my research posits that reality is not one specific thing, per say, but rather that there are two types of reality (objective reality and perceived reality) that work together to form what we know as the world around us.

So, to begin, due to the fact that this "agreed upon" reality, which, again, I call objective reality, may not be ultimately true, it actually falls on all of us to make it true. What I mean by this is that in order to truly establish an objective reality for any of us, we all must engage in a social contract wherein we all agree on an endless series of different measurable things. And as previously mentioned, this is the foundation for quite literally everything in existence, at least from a scientific perspective. I mean, what IS, is, because it IS, right? I.e., the sun is hot and ice is cold. When you press the accelerator of a vehicle that is functioning properly it will go forward, and right now you are currently looking at words written by a guy who just took an edible before this writing session. Anyway, what I am getting at is that at some point we all collectively agree upon and decide what makes up objective reality, and this makes it, for all intents and purposes, the real and/or true version of reality.

Of course, with this said, given that at this point in history we can still only interact with a mere morsel of the matter present in the universe, establishing an objective reality remains a very hard thing to do. Nonetheless, though, the scientific method and/or our own large-scale collective observations do give us at least somewhat of a framework for what is and isn't. Hell, if nothing else, the fact that we have achieved cognition, and therefore existence (I think therefore I am), gives us at least that as a foundation for the existence of a version of real and objective reality. I.e., the simple acts of thinking and speaking allow us to interact with the universe, which must mean that the universe, or at least something, is real. I digress though. To summarize this concept so that we can move on, we may know nothing more about objective reality than what we can interact with, and those interactions may be distorted, but either way it is a fact that we are actively influencing what is and isn't, so there must be an is and isn't that's objective, real, and true.

Ok, so moving on, even though I do believe in a real and quantifiable reality, or at least quantifiable to the best of my abilities, this is not the only type of reality I believe in. To explain, if I were standing in front of you right now and said to your face that you do not have hands, you would likely think me insane, right? In fact, it is highly likely that, when faced with this challenge, you would show me your hands, wave them around in frustration, and/or even smack me right across the face, should I continue to pester you, of course. Well, regrettably, it is to no avail. This is to say that, despite this emotional fit of protest, you have simply not convinced me that you have hands, and therefore, after succumbing to a loss of words you storm out of the room in a fit of rage.

Now, in your eyes this may be an absurd situation, but for a moment imagine a third party watching this interaction who isn't quite as traditional as you are. You see, to a third party observing this interaction, it appears that there are two possible options. I.e., either I am correct and all of you lunatics seem to think that the angry person has hands, or you and the angry man are correct, and

I am just a fool who got slapped across the face. Well, at this point everyone reading this would likely assume the latter was correct, yeah? But what if I am actually the one who's right? Well, I am obviously not, but bear with me.

Put plainly, I do not see any point in arguing about the existence of objective reality. I mean, as I just said, even if it is not ultimately true, nonetheless there is still a consistent side of reality that we all recognize as real. Be that as it may, though, there is also another side to this "what is real" coin, and this side is actually far more important to the framework outlined in this book than objective reality is. Let me explain.

In essence, in order for objective reality to exist, just as Hume pointed out, we need a series of shared experiences. Well, we do… ish have this, but since our shared experiences of objective reality are not ones that are empirically and/or ultimately true, at the end of the day our view of objective reality is contingent almost entirely upon our perceptions; and these perceptions are where people can have a ton of disagreement. I mean, if you don't believe me just go into a room full of diverse people and ask a couple of questions like, *is there a God, what happens after we die, is abortion murder,* and *who will win the Super Bowl in 5 years?* If you do, I will place my personal guarantee on the line to say that the room will rather quickly erupt into a frenzy of devout Christians battling dogmatic Atheists, feminists smearing menstrual blood on their faces and screaming while pro-life advocates say they hate puppies, and Eagles fans tackling anyone who doesn't like those fucking birds. In other words, what I am getting at is that when it comes to reality there is a grey area, and this grey area of, not what is, but rather what *may* be makes up what I call **perceived reality**; and this reality, mind you, is arguably every bit as "real," if not more so, than objective reality because, put frankly, unlike objective reality, this one can be bent and/or manipulated in ways that have a drastic effect on the world. All without ever even having to consider what is true.

You see, there is an old saying that goes, "Beauty is in the eye of the beholder," and I have even used this before myself over the years, especially whilst looking at some of the partners that my friends have shacked up with. I mean, I am not trying to be rude, but c'mon folks, we all have that couple we know where it just doesn't make any sense why one of them is with the other, right? Well, when it comes to situations like these, wherein two unlikely bedfellows end up together, at the end of the day whether I think my friend's mate is attractive or not is, in essence, completely irrelevant. Hell, whether their mate is a good biological specimen is even largely irrelevant, which shouldn't be the case given our biology. In other words, even if my friends' mate is objectively unfit, be it because of a low IQ or some disease that should, according to our evolutionary development make them unattractive to my friend, science and I be damned because the only thing that truly matters to my friend is what my friend sees when he looks at that aforementioned mate. Put another way, regardless of what is objectively true about my friend's mate, what really influences my friend's behavior is what their perception of that person is. Ergo, perceived reality may not be real and/or true in a technical sense, but nonetheless, you shouldn't sleep on it. Make sense? Great.

◄◦►

Alright, continuing on with this concept, as members of the human species we are incredibly good at deceiving ourselves and/or morphing our perceptions of reality into shapes that we find familiar, which suggests that the lens through which we see the world is subconsciously biased. In lay terms, we see what we want to see and dull any aspect of objective realities' truths that we don't like, and sometimes even convince ourselves that they are false altogether. I.e., *I see the best in other people because I believe this is all a big test from God, I ate another cookie because I deserved it, I only cheated on you because you cheated on me first and therefore, I did nothing wrong,* I mean for fucks sake where does it end? Well, unfortunately it never ends, and instead we must battle our own natural impulses to make a more comfortable false reality daily, lest we fall into cognitive dissonance, which is where we know things to be true, but deny them to ourselves, nonetheless. Anyway, my point is that our desire to see what we want to see, or at least our susceptibility to it, is a concept that can be, and often is, leveraged by skilled manipulators through the art of communication.

You see, at the end of the day everything we experience in objective reality, without exception, goes through our own mental filtration and refining processes, and what comes out on the other side may not be the same thing it was at the beginning. I.e., everything we experience in our life has the potential to be altered, either by ourselves, or more importantly for this book, by others. To explain, comedian Bill Burr had a great joke in one of his Netflix comedy specials from a few years ago called "Paper Tiger" wherein he was talking about his wife always being confused about where his outbursts of anger came from. According to Burr, his wife did not understand why he would become so spontaneously and irrationally angry at things that seemed so mundane. Well, in reply to this Burr goes on to tell a descriptive story about how he had been humiliated at Christmas one year by his father and made to act like a girl while being photographed, which, if I remember correctly, was a form of punishment for trying to guess what was inside the gifts. At any rate, at the end of Burr's story he looked out over the crowd and jokingly explained that perhaps, just maybe this contributed to his habit of "reading too much" into certain things and then getting irrationally angry over them.

What we can take away from this story is that every communication we experience, verbal or non-verbal, goes into our mind to be processed by our cognitive resources, gets cut with all the bullshit we have lived and/or experienced, and then, for better or worse, a reply comes out on the other side. And this reply, even if it is just silence, or even a physical action (which can both be non-verbal communications in certain situations), may not fit with or be appropriate for objective reality, as we saw with the Burr story, because the person replying in these scenarios may not be living in objective reality. I.e., they may, in fact, exist in their own version of perceived reality instead.

SIDENOTE

During my research I found that more often than not humans actually prefer perceived reality over its more "real" counterpart; and because of this, in order to be successful during my experiments, I ended up having to temporarily discard my tether to objective reality altogether so that I could instead focus on my participants perceived realities. This is something that you will have to learn to do as well, at least if you wish to manipulate others successfully that is, but more than that, it is also something that you should be aware of in case anyone tries to manipulate you. I.e., understanding how perceived reality works, and also how natural it is for us to choose this type of reality over objective reality (believing what we want to be true instead of what we know to be true), can help quite a bit when it comes to defending yourself against those who are actively trying to influence you.

Alright, moving on, as I have suggested before, whether it is philosophically true or not, humanity as a whole has come to agree on many truths about the world around us, and these truths make up the various tenants of objective reality. To expand upon this concept, when it comes to how this process of establishing objective reality actually went down, in essence, humans have created this framework for "what is real," in part, through storytelling over hundreds of thousands of years. What I mean by this is that, if you remember chapter one, then you remember that when we are communicating with each other we are simply manipulating one another. Well, in this chapter I want you to add another layer onto that and to also think of communication, not only as manipulation, but also as a form of telling a story.

To explain, just think about it. At the end of the day it really doesn't matter if what you are saying (or not saying) while communicating is fact or fiction, nonetheless, while communicating you are, essentially, creating a narrative that conveys something to the individual on the other end (the receiver). And this is an important part of the manipulative dance because this individual's return communication is significantly dependent upon the details and/or persuasiveness of the story you are sharing. Put another way, if you are successful in making a believable and persuasive story, you can adjust the reality of the person receiving it, and subsequently their response to that story. However, if you fail to do this, the opposite happens and now you become a threat who will be watched with extreme caution moving forward. AKA, you will be seen as a liar. Good to go?

Anyway, while on this topic it is also worth mentioning that these communicative stories do not have to be particularly lengthy and/or detailed, even though this is what we typically think of when we think of storytelling. This is to say that, yes, even mundane bits of information are, in a way, still a story. For instance, if my roommate asks me if I got milk on my way home and I reply with, "Yes, I placed a gallon of milk in the refrigerator," he can easily visualize me doing this, right? I mean, assuming he takes me at my word, presumably he will see me in line at the grocery store, getting home, fighting to unbag the milk from the plastic bag sticking to its sides from condensation, and then placing that gallon of milk in the refrigerator. Simple enough, yeah? Well, the truth is that when I told him about the milk, regardless of if I actually did the deed or not, in essence, I told him a story the same as if I had told him a lengthy diatribe about how I hunted and killed a mighty dragon named Basi to get the milk. In fact, the only structural difference between the nature of these two stories is that one is likely to be believed and the other is less likely to be believed.

SIDENOTE

Of course, some people would also say that the difference between these two stories is that the story about the dragon is a lie, but again, at the end of the day a lie is, essentially, just a story that is false. Plus, without more information, who can say, with confidence, that my story about the milk is actually true? I.e., what makes it true and the story about the dragon a lie other than the dragon story seems a bit more far-fetched?

Now, full disclosure, my research, which is outlined in this book, has established what aspects of a lie make it believable or not, so right now you don't have to know what makes these stories different. I just wanted to bring this up because, for now, I just needed to reiterate to you that a lie is just a false story with a manipulative purpose, and that this is true even if the lie is, as I will explain next, only one word.

To go a little deeper, in some instances even a single word can be a story. To use the milk scenario again, after my roommate asked if I had picked up milk earlier, if instead of a full sentence I had replied with a simple "yes," even though I did not actually purchase any milk, with just one word I have created a false reality in which, just like with the two longer stories, if he chooses to believe me, he now exists. In other words, whether I use a lengthy diatribe about a dragon, a short declarative sentence alluding to my trip to the grocery store, or even just a simple yes, in the end the result is the same and my roommates' perceived reality has temporarily changed. I.e., when I reply "yes" to his question, just like in the longer non-dragon version, after I communicate this one word story to him, he sees me texting in line at the same crowded store, driving home in the same little mom car, struggling in the same kitchen with the same clingy grocery bag, and opening the same refrigerator to put milk inside of it. Make sense?

Of course, be this as it may, when he does eventually go into the kitchen and there is no milk to be found my false story, regardless of its length, will fall apart, and so too will the perceived reality I have created; however, the fact remains that until the climax of this friction point, in essence, I have changed his objective reality by manipulating his perceived reality. Anyway, this may not seem that useful considering how innocuous this scenario is, but what if instead of a random "dude" my roommate was my significant other and getting this milk could actually be the straw that breaks the camel's back in terms of our relationship? I.e., what if this altering of their perceived reality allows me enough time to actually go get milk, thus allowing me to stave off a costly divorce? Can you see how this would be a big deal then? No? Well then how about a more sinister example, which, in all likelihood, is probably why you picked up this book in the first place…am I right?

To begin, what if I work with my roommate and we are both competing for a big promotion? Furthermore, what if that roommate is supposed to bake a cake for our boss's birthday party the next day? You see, in the above scenario, by creating a false reality, one in which my roommate incorrectly assumes he has access to milk, I have ensured that they will not have the necessary ingredients needed to bake a cake tomorrow morning, and therefore, will not be able to do this one "simple" task, a task, I might add, that will be noticed by our boss. Case in point, did my altering of their perceived reality, which affected how they behaved in objective reality, just make it so that I look better to the boss and/or have a better chance at getting the promotion? Any who, what I am getting at is that the ways in which altering someone's perceived reality can have an effect on objective reality are endless, but now that we are near the end of this chapter let's move on and tie all of these concepts up into a neat little bow, shall we?

To summarize and/or reiterate, if communication is just a form of storytelling, and if we communicate for self-serving purposes, then it stands to reason that communication at its very core is an act of manipulation that is inspired by our self-serving nature, and also one that utilizes storytelling. And this is true regardless of length, delivery method, and/or whether the intent/outcome of that story is positive or negative. Ergo, communication, it seems, assuming this premise is correct, is a constantly evolving dance made up of curated fact and fiction between at least two parties. Furthermore, if we are motivated by our self-serving nature, in this dance of storytelling there will always remain a constant pushing and pulling of personal agendas, much like two Muay Thai fighters locked in a brutal clinch, with one person always maintaining the dominant position. I.e., there is a purpose to the stories we tell in that all of them, without exception, are designed to create a desired response or outcome; and this inescapable reality of the communication landscape applies to telling a deceptive story to get out of a speeding ticket just as much as it does to giving your girlfriend an innocent compliment to make her smile.

So, what is real and does it even matter? Well, if the goal of communication truly is to manipulate others, and I think that we have established that it is, then in a way, no it does not matter what is real, only what is perceived to be real. I.e., take, for instance, a person with a severe mental disorder such as Schizophrenia. Let's assume for the purpose of this thought exercise that this person believes he or she is the holy prophet of God, and therefore, is charged by the divine with destroying all of the demons inhabiting our planet. Furthermore, let's also assume that this individual has even seen the demons in their dreams, and that this person knows without a shadow of doubt that these demons have red hair, freckles and threaten all of humanity! Thus, they must be slaughtered and burned so that humanity can be saved, and God can rule for 1000 years of peace and harmony!

Now, obviously this is fucking nuts. However, to the individual suffering from Schizophrenia, this reality is every bit as real, if not more so, than your reality as you sit here reading and/or listening to this book. Furthermore, if that individual with Schizophrenia decides to act on this perception of reality and starts killing gingers in the streets, well, then this perceived reality would certainly have an impact on the real and objective universe, would it not? Anyway, the point is this, perceived reality may not be "real," but it sure as hell can have a real impact on the world. I.e., when it comes to what is real, at least as far as a manipulator is concerned, you could either treat the individual with Schizophrenia, thus fixing their altered reality, or you could leverage their perception of reality in order to radicalize them. Got it?

Alright folks, we are almost at the end of this chapter, but before we go, I want to briefly share an excerpt from George Orwell's world-renowned novel "1984" that shows, once again, and in detail, how the skill of shaping perceived reality can be a very powerful "real-world" force. For context (Spoiler Alert), towards the end of the book the main character, Winston, has been captured by the thought police and is tortured/betrayed by every person he thought to be one of his closest allies. In other words, these friendships, for the most part, had actually been part of a carefully designed perceived reality that

was created to catch him committing treason against "The Party."
Anyway, that excerpt is as follows:

O'Brien was looking down at him speculatively. More than ever, he had the air of a teacher taking pains with a wayward but promising child.

"There is a Party slogan dealing with the control of the past," *he said. "Repeat it, if you please."*

"Who controls the past controls the future: who controls the present controls the past," repeated Winston obediently.

"Who controls the present controls the past," said O'Brien, nodding his head with slow approval. "Is it your opinion, Winston, that the past has real existence?"

Again, the feeling of helplessness descended upon Winston. His eyes flitted towards the dial. He not only did not know whether "yes" or "no" was the answer that would save him from pain; he did not even know which answer he believed to be the true one.

O'Brien smiled faintly. "You are no metaphysician, Winston," *he said. "Until this moment you had never considered what is meant by existence. I will put it more precisely. Does the past exist concretely, in space? Is there somewhere or other a place, a world of solid objects where the past is still happening?"*

"No."

"Then where does the past exist, if at all?"

"In records. It is written down."

"In records. And-?"

"In the mind. In human memories."

"In memory. Very well, then. We, the Party, control all the records, and we control all the memories. Then we control the past, do we not?"

Now I do recognize that this is an extreme example from a fictional story, though it grows less fictional by the day (Looking at you, Tech companies), however, it is nonetheless right on the money about the power found in the manipulation of perceived reality (If you don't believe me look up North Korea). Therefore, even though it is technically fiction, you should still take it as a potent warning, especially those of you that think this type of reality is just a "hoity toity" concept that you need not worry about.

Ok, we made it to the end everyone. In closing, as humans we do not necessarily have the ability to change the past. We can, however, control the present, which subsequently gives us significant influence over the future. Ergo, if perceived reality is malleable, and we live in a world of dupers and dupees, it is vitally important that we understand and master the art of manipulating this form of reality so that we can control and/or guide that future; and this is especially true when you take into account the fact that even now the media, government, corporations, and even everyone down to your best friends are already shaping the reality you exist in, whether you like it or not. Anyway, my point is that, with this grim reality in mind, I find it hard to argue against the idea that actively engaging in the formation of the world around you, even if that world is not ultimately true, is still far better than simply allowing yourself to be a pawn in someone else's reality, which will be the case if you sit passively by and decide *not* to manipulate the world around you.

Of course, with all of this said, unfortunately, constructing and/or altering perceived reality takes some time to master, but with that said, though, simply being conscious of the constantly evolving communication landscape we all live in is a good first step, and one that I hope this chapter has helped you take. I.e., you could call it the learning objective of this chapter. At any rate, though, my parting advice to you is to question everything around you and to examine it as objectively as possible because, as we just discussed, reality is always susceptible to change, and also because we are all inherently biased when we are trying to understand it (remember the Bill Burr story). Furthermore, assume that the people in your orbit will be doing the same, and that these people, even when they seem dull, are still rational, logical beings with agency who, despite their potential cognitive deficits, will still engage in the natural, self-serving dance of communicative manipulation the same way as everyone else, including you. And last but not least, since I brought up some pretty unsavory examples of manipulation in this chapter, let me just say that if these disturbed you, they shouldn't. This is because, again, you do not have to use this skill for sinister means. Rather, you can simply use it to control your own reality. In other words, if everything we do is self-serving anyway, which I have shown to be true, then using this knowledge for your own gain is no different than what you are already doing instinctively. The only difference now is that you are aware of it and can get better at it. Ergo, don't read into the morality of these teaching tools and instead just focus on the overall point? Good to go? Great.

Ok folks, that's it for this one. I hope to see you in the next chapter wherein we will be discussing baselines.

What is a Baseline

Opportunities? They are all around us ... There is power lying latent everywhere waiting for the observant eye to discover it.
—Orison Swett Marden

As mentioned in the previous two chapters, as a species we are very perceptive of our surroundings, and this applies to everyone, regardless of their IQ, level of formal training, and/or genetic heritage. Furthermore, we also discussed how humans have a very fine-tuned ability to recognize patterns within their environment (which includes other people's patterns mind you), and also that this ability to recognize and react to things that just do not seem right in that environment is an evolutionarily developed gift that has been a part of our genome since the cave days. Well, in essence, the reason we still have this ability to this day, despite most of us now living in relatively cushy, low-risk environments, is because the early individuals who did not have this natural ability likely ended up with their skulls bashed in thousands of years ago by keener cave dwellers. In other words, the cave dwellers who had this evolutionary gift survived during these harsh times and then went on to reproduce, thus passing on their genetic codes, which, among other things, contained all of this vital information. Then, as you may have guessed, that process repeated with the next generation, and so on and so forth until our species had, essentially, weeded out all of the members of our species who did not possess this trait.

Of course, even though this is how our species evolved over the course of our relatively short tenure, in our modern world filled with technology and comfort many people have lost touch with a large degree of our primal intuitions. Nonetheless, though, they do still exist within the deep recesses of our conscious/subconscious minds, and this is good news because, since they still exist, we can harness them and train them to be more acute. For example, a study was conducted by a coalition of researchers in the UK several years ago that looked at the Hippocampus' of Taxicab drivers in the bustling urban metropolis of London. Now for those who don't know, the hippocampus is the portion of our brains in charge of navigation, which, thanks to GPS, most of us have, unfortunately, lost touch with. In any case, these researchers were inspired to conduct this study because they had noticed that London cab drivers typically refrained from using GPS assistance, a difficult feat to accomplish considering the cities' outdated and over-congested infrastructure. Well, after asking a series of questions, these researchers discovered how competitive the taxi driver environment is, as well as how long it takes to become a proficient driver, typically 2-4 years, and as a result concluded that, because of these conditions, many of the drivers felt that the decision to memorize the ins and outs of the city without the aid of technology increased their chances of having a successful career.

At the end of the study the results showed that the vast plurality of cab drivers with over 2 years of experience had enlarged Hippocampus', at least this was the case when the scientists compared their brain scans to those of their civilian counterparts; and what this data suggests is that the London cab drivers, well, the ones who took the time to memorize the city that is, had quite literally changed the size and structure of their brains through nothing more than repetition. Furthermore, the research also showed that, even though the Hippocampus will reduce in size after a prolonged period of not driving, some permanent changes will still remain. This is to say that even though the driver's Hippocampus' did decrease in size after retirement, their Hippocampus' were still larger after their career than they had been before they started driving. And this remained true even after several years of inactivity. Pretty neat, right?

Overall, my point in bringing this example up is to say that, if this ability to change the structure, size, and subsequent functionality of one's own brain is possible for a cab driver in the posh urban core of London, why can't it be true for other primal functions of the brain that everyday people use? Well, I believe that it can; or at least that we can train our brains to perform certain inherent tasks more efficiently and effectively than they do currently.

SIDENOTE

The United States Marine Corps uses baseline training in their IED (Improvised Explosive Device) training. As one of the most elite fighting forces on the planet, I believe that they have a very practical and worthwhile definition of a baseline that will become important later on in the chapter. This definition is as follows:

"A baseline is a basis for comparison and a reference point against which other things can be evaluated. A Marine creates a baseline by looking at the current situation and determining the context and relevance of their observations. The Marine then measures that analysis against the template and prototypical matches (File Folders)."

Ok, moving on, in order to spot things that may be red flags, or things that just don't add up in your environment, you have to first establish what is called a baseline, and in lay terms, a baseline is the normal day-to-day environment, behavior, and/or atmosphere of any person, place, or thing. Now even though this seems like such an obvious concept that we would all be familiar with, especially after naturally learning to do things like read our parent's mood before asking for something or knowing when your significant other is pissed at you, despite them saying that "everything is fine," I actually first learned about this term in the United States Marine Corps. This is to say that, as a young Marine, referred to as a "Boot" due to being fresh out of "Bootcamp", you undergo hours and hours of arduous and repetitive training. You are required to relentlessly take weapons apart and put them back together, endlessly march and drill in the barracks or on official training grounds, and even take turns putting real tourniquets on your squirming comrades for hours on end; and the reason for this repetitive and seemingly unceasing training, which I did not fully appreciate until my first deployment (Iraq), is to familiarize yourself with the baseline of a combat environment so that, much like with the London cab drivers, you can recognize what is normal in your environment and what is not, thus allowing you to react quickly to any situation using only your muscle memory and instincts. At any rate, what I want to do now is to tell you about my own personal journey when it comes to establishing baselines, because I think this will help things make a little bit more sense.

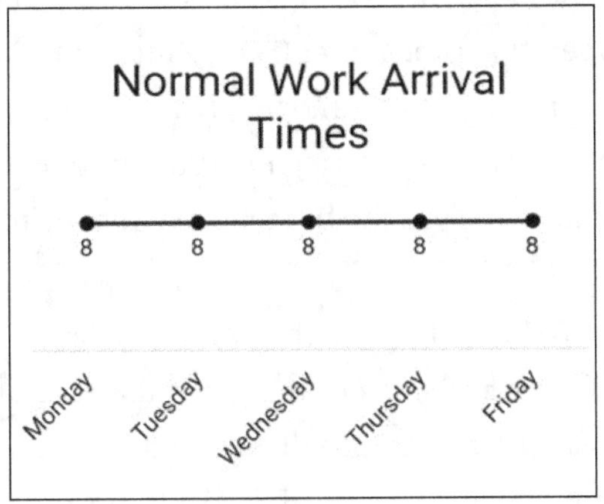

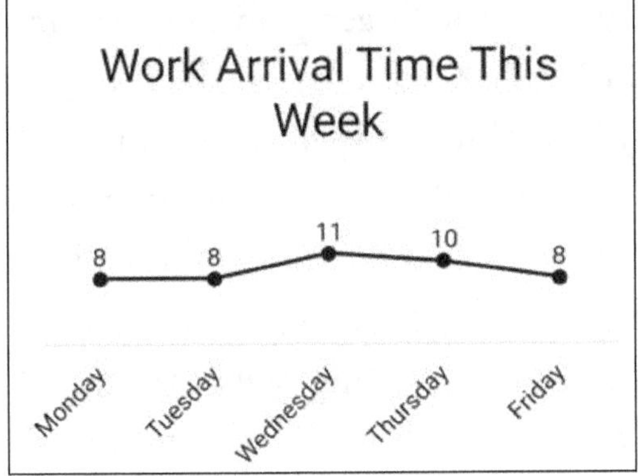

SIDENOTE

In the midst of the adrenaline dump fueled by a combat environment you have to be able to react without thinking. This is because in combat and other high-stress situations, something known as "The Chemical Cocktail," which is an amalgamation of fight or flight hormones, and endorphins that flood your system in times of duress, takes hold of you and makes thinking more difficult, fine motor skills non-existent, and can even lead to a full shutdown of your ability to move (Shell Shock). Ergo, constant training is the only way to drill the proper reactions and/or standard operating procedures (SOP's) into your subconscious so that, when shit does hit the fan, Marines, essentially, stop thinking and just act; and a major part of this training involves learning how to analyze the baseline of your environment.

When I first showed up to the Marine Corps fleet (AKA the actual Marine Corps and not a training battalion), most of my senior Marines had just returned from a deployment to Afghanistan, which is an environment with a very high IED (Improvised Explosive Device) threat. Well, given the geopolitics of that time, as a battalion, we knew that in less than a year we would likely be deployed to an area with a high IED threat as well (at the time I believe that it was either Iraq or Yemen), and because of this immediate need to train our brain's ability to spot IEDs, every morning the other Boots and I would be made to walk side by side around the barracks picking up trash, broken beer bottles, and cigarette butts.

Of course, as simple as this sounds, in reality, it wasn't. In other words, every time one of us would miss an item that needed to be picked up, which was easier to do than one would realize, a senior Marine would loudly declare "boom" while throwing a rock at the Boot who missed it. The Boot would then have to fall down and feign panic by writhing and screaming as if their leg had been blown off. Now, from a distance it must have looked ridiculous and almost comical as a young Marine rolled around begging for their mother while a senior Marine screamed and yelled in their face at the top of their lungs; but to us, it was a highly intense moment and one that the senior Marine would make even more chaotic and challenging if we hesitated for even one second.

Anyway, putting how it looked aside, once "boom" had been declared we had to immediately pull out a tourniquet, which we were required to carry on our persons at all times, and "save" our fellow Boot by placing the tourniquet tightly around their upper thigh. If we took too long or the tourniquet wasn't tight enough, which is difficult to achieve considering that during the process you have to use your shin to painfully clamp the Boot's femoral artery, the seniors would either make us start again, or even worse, make us "take contact." Now, starting over was bad enough in and of itself, but during these latter scenarios, however, not only did one Boot have to treat the casualty, but to make things even more complicated now the Boot's not putting a tourniquet on the injured Marine had to subsequently organize and engage a simulated enemy threat, which, of course, inevitably led to even more casualties until we were all dirty, exhausted, and/or dead.

Needless to say, I got very good at two things over these morning police calls. The first was putting on fucking tourniquets and killing invisible enemies. The second, however, was instinctively spotting and/or reacting to anything that didn't belong in the tan, sand-crusted rocks around our barracks. Ergo, through this repetitive training I had learned to establish a baseline of my environment, a baseline that, among other things allowed me to simply react based on muscle memory whenever there was a threat.

Now to avoid any more hazing than was necessary, put plainly, I became an expert at establishing a baseline of my barracks environment, and after a certain amount of time, I would say about 8 weeks, I began to notice every abnormality in the natural desert earth without even trying. Hell, this training, as simple as it was, had such a potent effect that I would even pick up random bits of trash during my free time purely out of habit. At any rate, this was a good foundation for my baseline training, and one that would become very useful when I eventually found myself in real combat environments, but my journey did not stop there; and as it continued, we ended up moving on to various field exercises, all of which upped the ante significantly.

Perhaps the most notable of these field exercises, at least when it came to IED spotting that is, was the illustrious Range 800 in Twentynine Palms Marine Corps Air Ground Combat Center. In essence, this range was a fully interactive range complete with Arab-speaking role players, fake black powder IEDs that actually exploded with nonlethal baby powder shrapnel, and even enemy combatants, who were dressed in authentic clothing and carrying simulation rounds that would leave one hell of a welt if they hit you. I digress though. My time at range 800 began by going through a strenuous cycle of classroom instruction led by then-retired vets who had decided to take up a training role. These "salt dogs" as we called them, were known as green shirts, and to put it lightly, they knew everything there was to know about IEDs. Of course, be this as it was, one can only be taught so much in a classroom, so in addition to these invaluable periods of instruction, we also got to, or rather had to, trollop out of the air-conditioned training trailers with all of our clunky gear into the hot June sun of the Mojave Desert for practical application training.

At first, this practical application training consisted of fairly simple IED lanes that followed a natural wadi system (basically a collection of miniature valleys). In other words, they were, essentially, just crude pathways made in the desert that we had to follow as a unit in order to practice our SOP's, the catch being that they were also riddled with baby powder bombs. This is to say that as we patrolled these little desert pathways, if we spotted an IED, or even an IED indicator (straight lines, unnatural colors, etc.) we had to go through a series of standard steps that the Marine Corps uses to deal with these types of threats, and, in lay terms, the objective was to patrol down the lanes and avoid getting blown up. Now, because I was a Boot and this was my first major range, much to my joy, at least after seeing how complex maneuvering a patrol in real life can be that is, I had only one, very simple job; do not step on a bomb. Simple enough, right?

Well, unfortunately, as fate would have it, this is actually easier said than done. At any rate, though, it was my job and I felt ready, however, as the beginning of the exercise grew nearer and we prepared to step off, I began to worry. So, to try and calm myself I tried to focus my mind on what had been taught during the periods of classroom instruction in the hope that this would lead to me not being the guy that blew everyone up.

Now, what I thought about in those moments may not be a ton of use to you in your day-to-day life, but I will share anyway because maybe, just maybe, you will find them to be relevant. To begin, when attempting to avoid stepping on a bomb, should you ever find yourself in that position that is, you want to look for things that do not occur naturally in nature, because these could indicate one of the many components of an IED or IED trigger. This is to say that straight lines, shiny objects, bright or fluorescent colors, perfect circles, etc. could all be signs of an improvised explosive device because these sorts of explosives are more often than not made out of household items. I.e., a blue patch in the dirt could indicate a kerosene jug filled with HME (Homemade Explosive) and a straight line across a road, or "ant trail" as we called them, could indicate a buried wire that leads to a pressure plate trigger. Oh yeah, and don't forget that, even though these cues are not a natural part of the environment, these abnormalities from the baseline are not always obvious, even when you are in the middle of nowhere. In other words, perhaps you are not operating in Iraq or Afghanistan, two countries replete with garbage and debris on nearly every road, back alley, and open patch of nothingness within their borders, but this does not necessarily mean that the area you are in is free from human trash either. So, keep an eye out and don't get complacent just because the last piece of debris wasn't a bomb. Anyway, let's get back to what happened at Range 800.

SIDENOTE

If you ever find yourself in an IED environment, you want to visually scan everything by looking right to left, not just left to right. The reason for this is because we are used to reading left to right as Americans. Therefore, we are more likely to glaze over things haphazardly while looking left to right. However, when looking right to left your brain slows down and pays more attention. Don't believe me? Have a friend go hide some household items outside from 5-50 yards away. Go outside, find a good spot adjacent to where they hid the items, and stay there. When you are settled into a good spot, see what you can spot by looking left to right, record it, and do the same thing while looking right to left. Which was more effective at finding hidden items? Just food for thought in case you find yourself trying to establish a baseline of somewhere unfamiliar, even if there are no IED's.

Ok, where were we? Ah, yes, range 800. So, once comm checks were complete and our squad-sized patrol (12-15 Marines) was staged in the proper order, with me being the third man from the front, we set off. Now as one may have assumed, given the circumstances, we went ridiculously slow at first, however, within a few minutes the green shirts told us that this is not the speed we would go on an actual patrol, and that if we didn't stop cheating, put plainly, they would blow us all up. Ergo, much to our chagrin, the patrol leader picked up the pace. Of course, my mood was still naively unaffected by this change because, again, I was the third man in the patrol which, in essence, meant that all I needed to do was mimic the footsteps of the man in front of me so that I did not stray off of the "cleared" path; but this sense of false security was, well, just that. False.

Moving on, at the five-minute mark we had made it about halfway (300 yards) down the system of small valley-like wadis, and for the most part things were going well. Unfortunately, though, this dull state of affairs was short lived and all of a sudden, around that 300 yard mark, the order to halt was given by the lead man in the form of a silent, palm forward, fingers together raising of the left hand; a signal that was then passed down the line of troops from man to the man until it reached the rear man in the patrol.

When the entire patrol had stopped, a second communication, just like a game of telephone with deadly consequences, was passed down from the front in the same man-to-man fashion, and this communication was a verbal confirmation of an IED at the front of the patrol. Now, even though I knew that this was just training, the environment was so realistic that my heart immediately began to pound. Especially so after I noticed that the green shirts had all moved from their nearby perch atop an adjacent highpoint and were now beginning to swarm us, all the while whispering to one another in hushed tones.

As they observed us the patrol leader began to move up the column while talking to a simulated tactical operation center (TOC) on the radio, and when he had reached the front of the patrol the order got passed down to move into the second C of the five C's of IED prevention (Confirm, Clear, Call, Cordon, and Control). This is to say that at this point the IED had, in fact, been confirmed, and therefore it was paramount that we establish a 360-degree perimeter of security and observation around the IED. Now, for those who aren't vets, just know that this didn't mean that we had to physically make a circle around the IED because, well, that would be extremely impractical. What it did mean, however, was that we needed to spread out to the upper edges of the wadi so that we could visually cover 360 degrees around the confirmed homemade explosive device. I.e., we didn't physically need to surround the explosive device, but instead just needed to make sure that we could cover all the way around it with our fire, should any enemies come into the area that is.

At any rate, I knew that this was the next step, but be that as it may, I was still extremely nervous and unsure of myself. So, I did what any good Boot would do. I looked around to see what everyone else was doing. Sure enough, like clockwork, everyone else in the patrol began to move toward the top of one side of the wadi or the other in a stuttered tac column formation, which basically means that one guy went left and the next went to the right so that our squad could adequately cover both sides of the area, and not wanting to get left behind, without looking I started to move up the wadi to my left.

Needless to say, the going was tough, not only because it was steep and the ground was sandy on top with a base layer of small, loose rocks underneath, but also because it was hot. Like 120+ degrees hot. Nonetheless, though, I continued on with steady, albeit sloppy movements, slipping and cursing the entire way. Well, when I was almost at the top of my side of the wadi, a milestone that should have meant a much needed rest, I began to notice a surplus of green shirts in my area, whom until now I hadn't noticed. And I also noticed that they were watching me intently.

Funny enough, this realization that I was being watched did not really have time to make me nervous because, just as soon as it came, I felt the ground under my left boot begin to give way. Now, if this had been a movie, you could say that this is the point in that film where the screen would have paused and a narrator would have come in and said something along the lines of "Yep, that's me. I bet you're wondering how I got here, right?" Well, this was no movie and there was no pause. Rather, as soon as I felt my boot losing its purchase, I also felt a slightly dulled crunch which was immediately followed by a boom that reverberated all of the way through my body.

Now, much to my surprise, this reverberating boom was actually all I felt. And I say that it was a surprise because what I had expected to happen was for a plume of sand and dust to explode around me followed by a painful blast of compacted baby powder. Thus, for a brief, and I mean very brief moment, I legitimately felt a tinge of relief because I had temporarily convinced myself that there had not, in fact, been an IED blast, but instead that some sort of random fluke had occurred. Well, as I said, this relief was rather brief because as I turned around to look at the rest of the patrol behind me, ignorantly pleased with myself that I hadn't actually done any harm, the senior Marine directly behind me, who was actually being bombarded by a shower of rocks and sand, went down on the command of the green shirts and began to scream.

"Ah! God damnit I'm hit. Fucking Jesus Christ where's my dick man? Where is my fucking dick?"

Strangely enough, as flamboyant as this display was, I didn't find it disturbing, probably because of all of our barrack's training. But what I did feel was a potent and immediate wave of embarrassment. Now, perhaps that makes me a narcissist, but truly, the main source of stress for me in that moment was not that a grown man, who also happened to be a trained and hardened killer mind you, was flopping around on the ground crying out about his missing member, but instead that I felt like the whole patrol was staring at me.

Well, as fate would have it, they were all staring at me, at least those who knew what came next, that is. In any case, despite my embarrassment-induced paralysis, the patrol leader, who had already been in situations like this in real life, snapped me out of my daze and screamed out an order.

"Nobody moves! Oakes, get to the fucking casualty!"

Now, again, for those who are not familiar with military tactics, this was not a form of punishing me, per se, but rather the most tactically sound next move. You see, because I had been the one to step on the pressure plate, thus triggering the IED behind me, I was simply the closest to the casualty. I digress though. Despite being immobilized at first, after his command I sprang into action, started running toward the casualty, who was about 15 yards away, and slung my rifle behind my back so that I could treat him without putting it down.

Due to my close proximity, by the time I made it to the senior Marine he was still screaming and writhing around. Now, I had trained this particular step enough at the barracks that I was able to react without thinking, but nonetheless, it was still extremely difficult because the entire time he fought me with his hands and hips, especially when I clamped his artery with my shin, which, as I said before, put an immense amount of pressure on his very sensitive femoral nerve. At any rate, despite his efforts at resistance, I was eventually able to get the tourniquet on.

After I had secured the tourniquet, I looked up to see what was going on. This was when I noticed that the rest of the patrol wasn't simply sitting back and watching, as I had assumed they were. Rather, most of the Marines were now preparing to do what is called a staggered egress, basically when the man in the back bounds to the front of the patrol while the others hold security, only to then signal to the new "rear man" that it was his turn to go. And as this was going on, the patrol leader was working on clearing a hasty landing zone (LZ) at the bottom of the wadi system where the landscape flattened out to open desert. So, needless to say I felt the tension of being center stage ease a little. Anyway, after a few moments of trying to calm down the now crying senior (In hindsight, I commend him for taking the training so seriously because it certainly amped things up, which, I suppose was the goal.) the order came to get the casualty up onto my shoulders and down the wadi system to the hasty LZ.

Now, in the movies it looks pretty easy getting a person up onto your shoulders and into the buddy carry position. In reality, it is a major bitch, especially when they do not want to go. Nonetheless, though, urged by a slew of encouraging comments from the other senior Marines in the area ("Get him the fuck up Oakes!" "Move your pussy Oakes!" God damnit Oakes if you don't get him on your fucking back right now, I am going to kill you, and then fuck your corpse like an Oceanside whore!") I got the flailing Marine on my shoulders with all of his gear and started booking it down the bottom half of the wadi, careful to only take the cleared path that was conveniently marked by shaving cream.

To say the least, and I hope I don't sound like a bitch when I say this, this part of the exercise was hard. Like, hard enough that if it wasn't so clearly expected of me, I would not have thought it was possible to do. I mean, together our gear alone weighed about 120 pounds, and on top of this, the senior was a pretty buff guy. I.e., he was probably in the 200-220 weight range, and this meant that I had to go about 500 yards, in 120-degree heat, across sandy and rocky terrain, all while carrying about 300 pounds on my back. So, yeah, suffice to say, whether I was or wasn't a bitch, by the time I reached the LZ my legs felt like Jell-O and I was so lightheaded that I thought I might actually drop the casualty. Luckily, this did not happen though, because once I was officially in the LZ the green shirts finally called index, which meant that it was time to stop, reset, and do it again. And do it again we did. Over and over and over and over and over again.

Skipping forward a bit, a few hours of patrolling and a lot of tourniquets later, a baby powder-covered squad of Marines returned to the training trailer for more classroom instruction. Now, for the record I know that telling you about these failures of the Marines charged with your national defense can be a bit alarming, but let me just say that ranges like Range 800 *are* designed for you to lose so that you can rehearse your standard operating procedures (SOPs). So, yes, our progress was nothing to write home about, but be that as it may, you would be surprised how quickly you can learn to establish baselines of an environment and even distinguish deviations in that baseline when you really start to train. Ergo, yes, we did encounter quite a bit of failure during these exercises, but having this ability to learn these skills in a non-combat environment only makes Marines that much more proficient in real-world settings. I digress though.

By the time we had made it back to the cool air conditioning of the training trailer I was beginning to "get it." I.e., I was becoming much better at being able to quickly recognize abnormalities in the baseline of my environment. And for me, this was a major win because, even though we did end up having more IED blasts during our training, I was not responsible for any more of them, which after all of the encouragement I received on the first patrol, was a relief. Well, unfortunately this feeling of relief, like the ones that had come before it that day (realizing everyone wasn't staring at me on the first patrol), was fleeting because after our next period of classes we were informed that for our next iteration of training we were moving over to the MOUT (Marine Operations on Urban Terrain) towns.

In essence, MOUT towns are full-sized villages and/or towns that the Marine Corps builds and then fills with fully furnished homes, trained civilian actors, and even trained enemy actors; and this complexity/interactive aspect of the training was extremely beneficial to us because, among other things, it gave us about as good of a simulation of the environments we would deploy to as you can get. In other words, and to put it mildly, they nailed it.

At any rate, as intimidating as this next iteration was, and it was very intimidating mind you, I was pleased when I found out that the green shirts were not complete dicks. This is to say that despite what I'm sure our commanders wanted for us (for them to launch everything they had at our meager squad), they didn't immediately throw us in the deep end, and for the first run of exercises, even though they did toss in a few gunmen, they excluded all of the civilian role players, which brought down the difficulty tremendously; however, even with this gift from the green shirts, these first MOUT town runs still went pretty much exactly the same as the earlier ones. Which is to say that they were a shit show. I.e., someone would get shot, go down, and then we would drag him into a building only to get blown up by another IED hidden in the doorway of that building. In any case, all things considered, this next training iteration might as well have been our first, despite the similarities it had to the first one, because even though I had developed a sufficient baseline of the rural desert environment, in a MOUT environment everything was made far more complicated by the addition of alleyways and windows from which crafty enemy actors can deal a lot of damage.

Alright, moving on, suffice it to say that things only went from bad to worse when the green shirts decided it was finally time to incorporate the civilian role players into the mix. When this happened, I was then not only expected to spot deviations in the baseline of my inanimate environment (dirt, rocks, doorways, etc.), but now I was also charged with spotting deviations in the atmosphere and/or body language of the people in that environment; people, by the way, who were not only speaking a language I didn't understand, but who also had on strange clothes that covered them from head to toe, thus making it rather difficult to perceive threatening body language and/or hidden suicide vests. So, yeah, let's just say that, given my inexperience with these situations at the time, adding in these role players to the training kicked things up a notch, and the result of this acceleration in difficulty was that most, hell, who are we kidding, pretty much all of my attempts to decipher friend from foe failed miserably (To any veterans reading or listening to this, don't worry, I was sufficiently hazed for my failures.).

Of course, even with all of these failures, the day was not without at least one bright spot. This is to say that, despite the seemingly endless loop of failure I had found myself in at Range 800, I did, however, manage to have at least one personal victory, which is a victory that I will never forget. To explain, we were on perhaps our fifth iteration of MOUT patrols, and we were patrolling up to a village that contained a busy market, or Souk as they are called in the Middle East. Now, for this particular patrol my days of hiding in the middle of the patrol were over, which was due to either enhance my training or, more likely, because the senior Marines were just plain tired of having tourniquets put on their legs (Because the lead man is often the first to die.). I digress though. During this run I was the point man which meant, in lay terms, that I was the canary in the coal mine should there be any hidden explosives and/or snipers in the area.

The first part of the patrol went quite smoothly and without incident, however, as I approached the market, I noticed two things that I deemed to be red flags. The first was the lack of people in the Souk. I.e., this normally busy market was empty and dead silent, which, according to our training (and previous failures) was a deviation from the baseline that indicated that the locals knew something was up. Now, even though I knew that we may be walking into an ambush, an IED attack, or a complex ambush (an IED strike followed by an armed assault), there was still no way to know for sure until we actually entered the village. So, we pressed on.

A few moments later the second thing that I noticed, and one that, even in a training environment sent a chill up my spine, was a man on a rooftop adjacent to the market. He had a cell phone in his hand, and it appeared to me, that he was recording us. Now, in addition to the first deviation in the baseline (the empty market), this made the situation even more suspicious, and because of this, I decided that it was worth risking some hazing to call the patrol to a halt, which I did using the same hand/arm signal that had been used during our first wadi patrol. Then, after the patrol had fully stopped, I reported what I had noticed to the man behind me, who subsequently passed it back to the man behind him, and so on and so forth until my message had made it all the way back to the patrol leader.

It took him a minute to get up to me, and with every moment I became more and more sure that he would call me a pussy and yell at me, but when he did finally make his way over to my area, I was pleasantly surprised that he actually agreed with my analysis of the villages baseline, and even gave me a pretty big compliment. "Hmmm. Good job not sucking as bad as usual Oakes."

In the end, these two deviations in the baseline were enough to make the patrol leader alter our course, and as a result, we actually ended up entering the town from the opposite side and avoided going into the abandoned Souk all together. Now, I am not going to say that I am the sole reason we did this, but I will say that by recognizing these deviations and subsequently stopping the patrol, I did give the leader of our squad enough reason to change our route, which resulted in us accomplishing our mission of reconning the town while suffering no casualties. So, I like to think that I at least played some part in the success of our patrol. At any rate, unlike our previous runs, which had all been proverbial blood baths, when the index was called on this one, I was ecstatic; mainly because this marked not only the end of the training day, but also our first successful MOUT run.

As I think back on that moment, despite being shot and blown up numerous times throughout the second part of the day, I was still happy and considered it a tremendous success. This is because, even though I had experienced a significant amount of failure, I had also learned an incredible amount about baselines. For example, as fate would have it, the same principles that apply to inanimate objects, such as unnatural desert terrain features and other IED indicators, also apply to humans.

Of course, simply realizing this connection is not enough in and of itself to be a skilled operator in a combat environment that involves a human element, especially when it is one that is not a carefully curated training environment wherein you know, albeit deep down, that no one is actually going to get seriously injured or killed. Put another way, even though I had made a great deal of progress in a relatively short amount of time, it would still take years of targeted training to really understand human baselines of behavior, if for no other reason than humans are emotional, unpredictable, and irrational. (Unpredictability and emotional behavior are things we will get more into during the next chapter when we talk about memory and the types of cognition processes). Anyway, in sum, this diatribe about the beginning of my own personal journey in this area is something that should give you newcomers to the manipulation game a little hope.

SIDENOTE

Another aspect of human behavior that makes this type of skill set so hard to master is that human baselines can also vary quite a bit based solely on the culture, region, and/or even the weather of an environment; and this is something that not only applies to Marines conducting combat and reconnaissance operations in foreign lands but also to people working normal jobs in the US (Think about a Californian trying to manipulate someone from rural Louisiana, or vice versa.), individuals doing business with foreign nationals, and individuals trying to work with and/or manipulate someone who has had a wildly different life experience than their own journey, even if they are technically from the same environment (Two black people, one from the hood and one from prep school). Be this as it may, though, the good news is that even if you are far from a master when it comes to understanding unfamiliar environmental/human baselines you can still get somewhat proficient at this process rather quickly, as I did with the Souk patrol.

Alright, continuing on, just to give you a taste of why this topic is important, during my research I found that the best time to manipulate someone is when they feel that they are in a position of power over you. Ergo, if you understand their baseline, as well as yours, you can adjust the baseline of the environment that you both exist in subtly, thus altering their perceived reality and making it easier to give them the illusion that this is the case and that they are, essentially, in control; and even better, if you do this process properly, which requires a thorough and, more importantly, accurate baseline analysis, put plainly, they will be oblivious to your influence. Hell, most of them won't even know how to look, which just makes this method, and the use of the baseline principle, all the more potent. Make sense?

Ok, so full disclosure, this baseline manipulation strategy is exciting stuff and ties into what I am calling the "sexy" part of this book (the second half), but it can also be rather complex. So, for now, the important thing for you is to just understand what a baseline is and to start practicing the skill of establishing them. This is to say that, at this point in time, the key takeaway is that a baseline is simply the homeostatic norm of whatever person, place, or thing you are observing. I.e., the baseline of a grocery store is different from the baseline of a doctor's office, and the baseline behavior of a 40-year-old woman from Wisconsin is very different from the baseline behavior of a 22-year-old man living in New York City. So try to pay attention to the specific baseline of your environment/ subject. What are the constants of your surroundings? Do you have quiet neighbors or loud neighbors? Is the parking lot normally full, or is it normally empty? Do these things change depending on what time of day it is? What time do you normally leave your house, and what time do you normally return? Who are the regulars in the places you visit, and who looks like they don't belong? Has that homeless man outside of your apartment complex always been there, or is he new? You see, taking a mental note of all these details, and anything else you can think of for that matter, can help you get a rough idea of what your environment normally looks like, and this familiarity with that environment is essential if you wish to form and/or mold your own objective reality by altering the perceived realities of others.

Now, even though we are starting out with baby steps (establishing a baseline of your current environment), to give you something to look forward to, the real power comes when you can do these same baseline analyses with people. I.e., is your boss normally in a good mood or a bad mood? When does his mood change? Is it the time of day or external stimuli like coffee, lunch, and/or when he is around beautiful women that his mood changes? What things is he interested in? Is he married? Is he gay? Does he talk negatively about other people in the office? If so, what are the things he critiques, and how can you find out what aspects he does and does not like about you? All of these things are very important, and the better you get at making observations like these, the more likely you will be to pick up on the subtle clues that forecast their thought processes, moods, and behaviors. Ergo, once you develop this skill you will not only be able to predict their behavior more accurately, but you will also be able to communicate with them in specific ways that aid you in accomplishing your manipulative objectives. But we will get more into that later.

SIDENOTE

Validity is a term that refers to the accuracy of findings. There are two main types of validity in the scientific community: **Internal Validity** and **External Validity**. According to *Research Methods for the Social Sciences* by Frederick J Gravetter & Lori-Ann B. Forzano,

"Internal validity is concerned with factors in the research study that raise doubts or questions about the interpretation of the results. A research study is said to have internal validity if it allows one and only one explanation of the results."

In other words, internal validity means that the findings are accurate within the context of the study. I.e., using the proposed findings from chapter two that Democrats smoke more than Republicans, in order for that study to have internal validity it is required that all of the other factors that may or may not influence why people smoke have been accounted for. Otherwise, the study is not structurally sound, and therefore does not possess internal validity. Got it? If not, then I guess you should watch a YouTube video on validity, or maybe do a little Google deep dive. Dealers' choice.

According to that same aforementioned source,

"External validity concerns the extent to which the results obtained in a research study hold true outside that specific study."

In lay terms, external validity is established if the findings of the study are true outside of the laboratory setting. I.e., in the example of the smoking study, external validity would not be achieved if months prior to getting their smoking habits measured the participants were regularly exposed to in-depth presentations regarding the dangers of smoking, which is something that most people in the real world would not receive before deciding whether or not to continue smoking. Ergo, in order for a study to have external validity, it must not conduct itself in a "fake" environment. Rather, it must possess similar conditions to the "real world," otherwise researchers cannot rely on its real world relevance, AKA, external validity.

Ok, we are almost at the end folks, so stay with me. In closing, the validity of data regarding "how to" and how accurate one can be at predicting human behavior has led to many heated debates among the scientific community, the military intelligence community, and cadres of behavioral psychologists; and two of the keenest minds in this debate are Mark Lowenthal and Bruce Bueno de Mesquita. Now, I don't have time to go too in-depth on these two gentlemen here, but in essence, Lowenthal is a well-known intelligence community veteran who believes that there is inherent uncertainty in every prediction we make regarding human behavior, and because of this, Lowenthal believes a more hands-on method is needed to understand humans, from a behavioral perspective that is. This is to say that, according to Lowenthal, intelligence is best gathered through close and/or personal relationships, which is why he is best known for focusing intelligence experts' training on zooming in close to the individuals they wish to know more about. In other words, when you know a person as a person, and not just as a mark, according to Lowenthal, you can then efficiently adapt to their communications instead of spending time and resources attempting to predict their communications.

Now Bruce, however, is on the opposite side of this debate. To elaborate, as a political scientist, what he believes is that we actually can use a scientific approach to predict human behavior by tracking and analyzing large swaths of intelligence data through a method known as a "collection swarm," which, in lay terms means getting as much info as possible about a demographics baseline and then analyzing that data for common trends. Of course, Bruce does still concede in his writings that there will always be unpredictable aspects of humanity, but nonetheless, he does make a good case for the idea that in our modern day and age we can get accurate enough data to make his "zoomed out" method worth pursuing. Anyway, the reason I brought these up right here at the end is because, in my analyses, I would say that both views hold some truth and that you should never abandon a manipulative resource. Ergo, if you never think about these two men again (though you should give them a quick internet search) just remember that there are several ways to approach establishing human baselines (up close and personal/zoomed out and impersonal), and both of them are not only valid, but also tools that you can and should use, depending on your specific situation/goal that is.

Ok, to tie a neat little bow on this, regardless of the accuracy with which we can/cannot predict human behavior, without a baseline of activity, one thing is certain. That is, when it comes to manipulation you will absolutely fail when trying to deceive and/or manipulate someone you see regularly if you have not accurately accessed and established their behavioral baseline. Worse than that, though, without this skillset when they are manipulating you, which we do instinctively when we communicate, you will not know it and will thus become their dupe.

Ok, in closing, for real this time, with all these things in mind my parting words to you are that learning to establish baselines and/ or predict behavior and then practicing those skills until you can visually play out an entire day in your head somewhat accurately is necessary before you can effectively utilize the framework outlined in this book. To that end, a drill that I do in order to hone/maintain these skills, and one that should not be too difficult for you to do, is to pick someone I know reasonably well, or whom I am at least familiar with. Then, after I have chosen my subject, I systematically go through a conversation with that person in my head while playing both sides, picking both subjects I discuss frequently, such as politics and baseball, and also ones that I rarely bring up, like fashion and pets. Then, after running through these conversations in my head, sometimes more than once, I try to actually have them in real life with the individual I chose.

Now, I am sure you will be clunky at first, especially if you are not naturally gifted when it comes to communication, but if you do this drill consistently, I imagine that you will be quite surprised how close you can get to predicting their responses. And when you do, the great thing about this drill is that, once you are proficient at it, you can easily add a level of difficulty by simply trying to branch out and see what alleyways you can/cannot take the individual down. I.e., if you want, you can ramp things up by trying to manipulate them into believing you about things that are not true while also trying to predict their responses; and it doesn't necessarily have to be big things or even important things either. For instance, maybe you make up an entire weekend you didn't have, keeping it believable and within reason of course, and then you see if you can get them to bite. Or maybe you convince them that you are a fan of a sports team that you actually loathe. However you choose to go about it, at the end of the day, while doing this drill you are still working out those brain muscles that we use every day when we weave our webs of manipulative stories (Again, we have talked about the ethics behind this. You are not a bad person for taking control of this process, which is already happening whether you accept it or not.).

SIDENOTE

An added benefit to making this drill more difficult is that when you learn how to weave and use a proper manipulative web you will already have some experience remaining calm while telling your manipulative stories in real scenarios with real consequences.

Alright, that's it for this one. Now let's move on and talk about human memory and some of the different aspects of our cognition processes.

What is Cognition

A word devoid of thought is a dead thing, and a thought unembodied in words remains a shadow. — **Lev S. Vygotsky**

So far in this book we have talked about morality, our self-serving nature, right vs wrong, what reality is, how there are two versions of it, and also, in the last chapter, what a baseline is and how to establish one. These topics are fairly broad in that they do not give you, the reader and/or listener, a lot of actionable data to use. Well, not when it comes to manipulating your environment through communication that is. Nonetheless, though, these abstract parts of the book, in my view, were necessary to include because they are still key foundational elements of the manipulation process. Ergo, without a sturdy foundation built upon these, I felt that the more material parts of the book would be, essentially, ineffective.

With that said, I do have to warn you that we still have one more chapter's worth of abstract stuff. This next chapter is that chapter and it discusses, among other things, a few more final foundational elements of my research. In that sense, I suppose you could call this chapter the bridge between the unsexy and sexy parts of the book. At least in the sense that this chapter is where we start to get into how manipulation actually occurs. But in any case, because this chapter covers things that may be less interesting and/or slightly drier than what we covered in the last chapter, at least to some of you, I am going to keep it as short as possible; but be that as it may, right off the bat, I do want to let you know that the next chapter, which covers the actual academic models of persuasion, will be much better understood if you read this chapter first, in its entirety. The reason, persuasion involves many factors and can be done in many ways, but at the end of the day, all of the models of persuasion still rely on using and/or manipulating the cognitive processes of others. So, again, it would benefit you greatly to first understand what cognition is, how memories are stored, and how these processes work together to inform your evaluations of your environment. Fair enough? Very well. Then since all of that is out of the way and you know why this chapter exists, let's get into it.

As someone who holds a graduate degree in political psychology, and who is currently pursuing a PhD in clinical psychology, I have become very familiar with the term cognition; but for the layman, cognition is an amalgamation of physical and mental processes that allows us to acquire information. In other words, it is the combination of mental processes that allow us to make sense of our physical surroundings. Now, even though that definition sounds simple enough, it is important to note that this amalgamation of processes involves more than merely interacting with our environment through the use of our five senses. A camera, for instance, can take a picture or even record a video of an object, but it is not, itself, necessarily doing anything with that information. I.e., the camera is not aware of the object, it does not have an opinion about the object, and it is not going to feel anything at all, good or bad, toward that object. Humans, on the other hand, when exposed to that same object will process the information that their eyes are giving them, cross-check this information with their current knowledge about the object, make an evaluation of the object based on this amalgamation of information, and then store that new evaluation for immediate and/or later use. In essence, this act of physically and mentally interacting with the object is cognition and it is how we process, understand, and store our observed experiences. Make sense?

In this chapter we are going to talk about, among other things, the four stages of cognition, the two types of memory, some theories that help show how both of these concepts work together to influence our evaluations of the world around us, and also some barriers to proper cognition that are relevant to the manipulation process, in that they all have the dichotomous ability to either help or hinder your use of it.

SIDENOTE

I use the term "object" in this chapter because this simplifies the process of teaching you about cognition. However, you should know that when I say "object" this can refer to an experience, person, sound, sensation, or anything else that our five senses allow us to interact with; and this is because, as I said before, our cognition is the process through which we interpret the world around us (objects) and make evaluations of it. So, do not get lost when I say "object." This is simply referring to whatever part of objective or perceived reality your cognition is currently processing.

To begin, there are several different academic schools of thought (models) that detail how we use our cognition, but all of these still agree on several basic stages of the cognition process. To explain these I will be using information gleaned from the writings and lectures of Dr. Fabian Neuner, Dr. Kathleen M. McGraw, Dr. Marco R. Steenbergen, Dr. Milton Lodge, Dr. Pamela Johnston Conover, and last, but certainly not least, Dr. Stanley Feldman (Check the references section for their works!).

The first stage of cognition is the **exposure/attention** stage. Put plainly, this stage of cognition occurs when our five senses interact with the object and/or experience in question. To use the example above, this stage would be when your 5 senses first see the camera, touch the camera, feel the camera, hear the camera, or, if you are a weirdo, taste the camera. Now, the level of processing power your mind will expend at this stage, at least in relation to that specific object, depends upon your level of exposure to it and how much attention you pay to it. This is to say that if you casually walked past the camera, as opposed to stopping and observing it closely, you would have far less informational ammunition for your cognitive processes to turn into an evaluation because your senses would have very little time to gather raw data. If instead, however, you were to pay a significant amount of attention to the camera, as opposed to simply walking by it, let's say you stopped and thoughtfully stared at it for a minute or two, this would increase the cognitive attention and cognitive effort that your mind would put toward the camera. Thus, in this latter scenario, your five senses would be directed to collect a lot more raw data about the camera than in the first, but either way, both scenarios take place in the first stage of cognition.

The second stage of cognition, which occurs almost simultaneously with the first, but not quite, is the **encoding** stage; and in essence, this stage is a preliminary stage of cognition, wherein the neurons in your brain simply make sense of what your 5 senses are telling you. To elaborate while using the camera scenario again, after you have been exposed to the camera and chosen to pay attention to it, during the encoding stage your mind would translate that raw data your five senses collected into the experience of seeing a black camera, recognizing that it is turned on, being aware that it is recording, documenting that it is approximately 8 feet away from you, etc. In this way, you can think of it as an organizational stage that interprets the information you gathered in the first stage.

This stage happens naturally and is not, per se, controlled by your active mind. Instead, it is more like a series of immediately available bits of information being sorted through and understood by the involuntary worker bee neurons of your mind. Think of it like the difference between your beating heart, which you have no, or at least very limited control over, and moving your legs to walk, which is a conscious and active decision that involves you proactively telling your brain to tell your legs to walk. Make sense?

Now, when it comes to this stage of the cognition process, it is worth noting that the speed with which this stage of cognition happens relies heavily on your levels of preexisting information regarding the object and/or experience. In other words, if you have seen a camera before this is going to help the encoding phase along by giving your brain a frame of reference, almost like a series of cheat codes, from which it can pull already encoded and evaluated data. Conversely, though, if you were from a third-world country, and not our modern tech-driven environment here in the United States, then your brain would need to start from scratch, and thus the encoding stage would end up taking more time/cognitive effort.

SIDENOTE

By evaluations I mean, in lay terms, what you think about an object, or rather what your attitude is about it. I.e., I love cameras, and this is an excellent model that has recording capabilities and lots of slots for memory cards so that it can record for hours (positive evaluation); or I hate cameras, and this one especially sucks (negative evaluation).

Continuing on, the third stage of cognition is the **evaluation** stage, and this stage occurs after you have been exposed to an object, and your mind has interpreted what your five senses have to say about it. Now, even though this stage sounds very similar to the last one, it is actually much deeper than the encoding stage in that it directly influences your attitudes and behaviors. This is because the evaluation stage is where you take the experience you processed from the raw data during the encoding stage, and turn that data into an actual evaluative judgment. I.e., if you see a camera in your home as you walk by, and you know what it is, what it does, that it is turned on, and also that it is pointed at you, all of which happened during the first two stages of cognition (exposure/attention and encoding), then you can make an evaluative judgment based upon this inputted data.

To illustrate, depending upon how you feel about being filmed by this particular camera, which is dependent upon what is going on in your mind in relation to the camera-specific information you encoded, as well as your past experiences with filming, this could spur you to either make a negative or positive evaluation of the camera. In other words, did your significant other put the camera in the room for an added layer of home security, and therefore, it is a positive thing that you prefer to be there; or do you live alone, and the camera means that someone is watching you, which we can all agree is both a creepy thing and probably a negative one? Either way, in both of these scenarios your subsequent behaviors and thoughts will be determined by your evaluations of the camera during this stage of the cognition process. I.e., if you make a positive evaluation of the camera, you will leave it on or maybe even change its batteries so that they are fresh; however, if your evaluation was a negative one you may instead run over, turn it off, and/or even call the police. Good to go?

SIDENOTE

Even though cognition is explained as occurring in stages with storage being the final stage, these stages interact with each other in different ways depending on your levels of exposure to an object, how much attention you pay to the object, how familiar you are with the object, and what type of memory you use when evaluating the object. This is to say that you should not think of these stages as ordinal steps in the cognition process but rather as aspects of cognition that work hand in hand in different ways at different times in order to establish an overall evaluation of an object and then store it. Then, when the cognition process is complete and you have this final evaluation, it will subsequently be used to determine your follow-on attitudes and behaviors regarding that object.

Ok, so the fourth and final stage of the cognition process, which often works in tandem with the third, is the **storage** stage. Now, in regard to cognition, and specifically how the storage stage is used, a great deal of pre-1980s academic literature believed in something called the rational choice theory. In essence, this theory posited that humans are rational and aware beings, and because of this, researchers who believed in the rational choice theory thought that humans always had access to all of the information within their minds. In other words, according to the rational choice theory, as you see the camera all of your past experiences with cameras and any prior evaluations related to cameras are immediately accessible and become part of the evaluation process.

As our understanding of cognition has improved, researchers in the social sciences have determined that this is actually false. The reason, regardless of the levels of exposure you have to the object and/or your brain's inherent level of processing horsepower (IQ), on a day-to-day basis we simply take in far too much data to be able to keep it all accessible and ready to use at all times. In light of this realization, modern models of this stage of cognition have adapted to now suggest that we actually have two types of memory storage, and this is now the standard theory, even though it is technically still debated which type of memory storage is more prevalent. Anyway, regardless of which answer is correct when it comes to what type of memory is used more often, the existence of two types of memory is nonetheless widely recognized as a legitimate theory among modern social scientists and is the theory that I will teach you about in this chapter.

So, when it comes to the storage stage of cognition, the first type of memory, or long-term memory (LTM) as it is called, is one that stores memories deep within the recesses of our cognition for future use. To illustrate, you can think about this type of memory as a storage facility inside of your mind that allows your cognition to take all of your evaluations and store them in neat little bins that are marked by a serial number and/or color code. Put another way, these memories are safe within your mind and can be accessed at any time if you expend enough cognitive energy looking for them, but they are not easily accessible and/or ready to use.

An example of long-term memory would be asking someone who does not keep up with politics what they think about the current president's policies. You see, even though they may not rigorously keep up with politics, and therefore do not have a lot of evaluations of them readily at hand, it is still highly unlikely that the individual knows literally nothing about the sitting president. So, in order to make an evaluation of the president's policies that individual would have to go into their mind's memory storage facility in order to retrieve information from their LTM that is related to the topic, which, in this case is the current president and his or her policies. Ergo, using this type of memory (LTM) in this situation would still allow the individual to make an evaluation of the current president even though they are not familiar with politics; but as you can see it would also require a good deal of mental time and energy because the memories are stored and not readily available.

Now the other side of this coin (the second type of memory), which is referred to as on-line or working memory, is one that keeps certain memories salient or more readily available. In other words, unlike LTM, when we are using our on-line/working memory our prior evaluations are very accessible and available for immediate use. To illustrate this type of memory, instead of a large storage facility, think of this model more like the back room of a bookies shop at a horse track. I.e., in this shop new evaluations of the horses (objects) are constantly pouring in, such as which horse is healthy, which horses have won a lot of races recently, which of the horse jockeys got drunk last night, etc.; and this constant influx of new information subsequently causes the bookie to keep a running tally of the status of the horses, which he uses to adjust the odds (their evaluations of the horses) accordingly. Simple enough, right?

Well, to bring this full circle, when it comes to the example of a person being asked what they think about the current president's policies, if instead of being a political outsider who had to use his LTM to make evaluations of the president, the individual who needed to make that evaluation was actually a working political analyst, they would likely have a quick and well-established answer for you when asked. This is because instead of having to go into their mind's storage facility, spend the mental time and energy to find the correct bin, and then check it out, they simply have to look to the most current odds (evaluations) on their bookie board.

As you can see, what type of memory is being used directly relates to the individual's prior knowledge of and/or exposure to the object. But to add to this, what type of memory is being used during the cognition process is also interesting in that it can actually influence when the evaluation takes place during the cognition process.

Without getting too far into the weeds, when long-term memory is being used during cognition the evaluation takes place only after a careful review of prior acquired knowledge. For example, if a person is asked how they feel about a particular political candidate, according to the long-term memory model of cognition (which you can find an excellent breakdown of in a paper called *A Simple Theory of the Survey Response* written by Dr. John Zaller and Dr. Stanley Feldman in 1992) they will stop, retrieve memories about that candidate, and also prior evaluations of that candidate that have been stored. Then, after a careful and cognitively robust review they will make a thoughtful evaluation of the candidate. However, if they were using the on-line/working model (which has been broken down extensively by Dr. Milton Lodge, Dr. Kathleen M. McGraw, and Dr. Patrick Stroh), since the mind of the individual who was asked to make an evaluation has been keeping a constant tally of the candidate over the course of the current election cycle, they would have a quick and almost immediate answer. In other words, as new information has been inputted over the election cycle, just like the bookie getting new juicy gossip about the condition of the horses and their jockeys, the individual's overall evaluation of the candidate would have changed with it and that new evaluation would have stayed at the front of their mind in their on-line/working memory. So, if the individual was using their on-line/working memory during the cognition process, their evaluations would have been continually updated and the most current would be, in a way, already established and available to use; and this would make the final evaluation of the candidate a quick one to retrieve and their response to you, therefore, would likely be relatively instant.

Now, to put all of that into lay terms, essentially, in the long-term memory model evaluations take place after the storage stage. This is to say that when this type of memory is used during cognition the memories are called up to the forefront of your mind from deep storage, an evaluation is made, and then the mind stores this information back in its appropriate place within your mental storage facility. On the other hand, in the on-line/working memory model evaluations take place during the storage stage because as your cognition is tasked with making an evaluation it will cross reference any new information about the object that you have recently encoded with the already accessible information you have on hand in your on-line/working memory. Your cognition will then make an evaluation, and after that it will then keep that new evaluation in your on-line/working memory where it is ready to use the next time you are asked to think about the candidate.

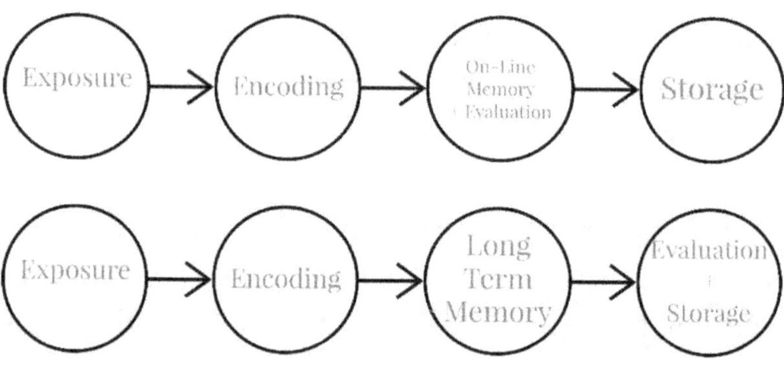

Alright, does that count as not getting in the weeds? I only ask because I could feel that rabbit hole getting away from me. In any case, I digress. As I stated earlier, the prominent academic literature on this subject competes between these two views of memory based cognition models. For this reason, and to tie a neat little bow on this section, I want to add in here the caveat that I, as well as a growing number of young academics, actually prefer a newer hybrid-style model of the storage stage wherein the level of exposure to and attention we give an object influences the specific memory model that our cognition will choose to use. In other words, we use both.

To explain, a political junkie like me would likely use the on-line/working model when asked to evaluate a candidate because I have a ton of exposure to politics and am constantly updating my evaluations of the political landscape. However, if I were to step away from politics for an extended period of time I would likely need to slow down and really think hard about the candidates before making those same types of evaluations. But nonetheless, in both scenarios I may still end up gathering some information from each type of memory. For instance, in the first situation I would likely end up digging deep into my memory storage for extra information if the person I was talking to wanted a very thorough and well thought out answer, even though I already have a lot of information about the object in my on-line/working memory. Conversely, in the latter scenario I may not have a ton of up to date information to use, but I would still have a baseline of relevant political knowledge in my on-line/working memory from which I could gather relevant information that would enhance my overall evaluation, which would primarily come from my LTM. Get it?

Because I believe that in addition to using both types of memory at different times most of the time we actually use both simultaneously, this hybrid-style model appeals to me way more than the traditional models. Of course, I have gotten a lot of pushback on this from certain individuals in the academic community, but my reply is simple. In essence, during previous experiments it just appears that only one type of memory is being used because, depending on the specific object, we may have more or less preexisting information available. Therefore, when making different evaluations about different objects we may heavily favor one type of memory over the other during each specific situation.

Anyway, I will dismount my intellectual soapbox now. Moving on, despite my own personal views on memory storage, in summary, the currently accepted theory is that LTM is used to make evaluations in more pointed and specific ways, whereas on-line/working memory is like the ram of your computer. This is to say that it is constantly receiving input and updating your evaluations based upon that input.

This overall framework regarding the storage stage is widely accepted and also ties into two concepts called the associative network model theory and affective intelligence theory. These two concepts are what I want to look at next because they should help explain in a little more detail how all of the stages of our cognition work together to form our evaluations of objects, which, as I said before, directly influence our follow-on attitudes and behaviors regarding those objects.

SIDENOTE

As I sit here writing this chapter and think about everyone who is reading and/or listening, it strikes me that you have all probably noticed that the evaluation stage of cognition keeps coming up, even whilst talking about the other stages. You would be right in noticing this. I say that because the evaluation stage, in essence, is where the rubber meets the road during cognition, and therefore may be the most important of the four stages, at least as far as the manipulation process is concerned that is. But enough about the individual stages of cognition, for now anyway.

Since by now you know the general workings of the cognition process, I want to keep building on this information and talk about something called the **associative network model theory**, which, put technically, is a framework for how our cognition uses the information we encode and our memories to make evaluations (I.e., this theory details how the cognition process actually looks and functions in real life.). You see, the associative network model theory suggests that each individual object we are exposed to over the course of our life exists as a node in a network of nodes within our minds and memories. To that end, you can think of this like a fencepost with the name of an object on it standing erect somewhere in a large field, with the field being your mind. When your 5 senses are exposed to this object this node is then triggered and lights up. So, in the instance of the camera, when you are exposed to the camera, choose to pay attention to it, and then encode the information your 5 senses are giving you about the camera, the camera node in your brain is activated, and your cognition is now focused on it and actively processing it.

Ok, so that is all fine and dandy, but what is important to know for our purposes is that this activated node does not exist in isolation. Staying with the field analogy, I want you to now imagine many different fence posts, each with their own name, planted firmly in the ground around that first post. Some are closer and some farther away, but they all have a wire that connects them to the post at the center. Now, even though all of the posts are connected to the first one, imagine that the closer a post is to that original one the thicker and more robust the wire connecting them is. This is very similar to what an associative network model is, and it is an inescapable fact that we all have one. Of course, this isn't a bad thing though, because they are a very important tool we use while making evaluations. I.e., all of the different nodes connected to and surrounding the first one become activated, albeit to differing degrees depending on their distance to the first one and the thickness of the wire connecting them, when the center node is activated; and in essence this means that these extra, or supplementary nodes as I call them, increase our ability to process information about the center one.

To put this into a clearer perspective, at the beginning of the chapter when I talked about seeing a camera in my home, during that experience my camera node was triggered and activated. After this, my mind activated a series of related nodes based on my prior memories and evaluations. For example, if I had recently had a very bad experience with a camera, that experience would have come to mind with greater strength than say a pleasant memory of taking photographs as a child, even though both would ultimately be present and accessible, because both would be connected to my camera node. Make sense?

Now what is interesting about this theory, at least from a manipulator's perspective, is that in addition to these positive or negative prior evaluations a plethora of other nodes could be activated at that same time. In other words, if the media coverage I had seen recently had been covering government surveillance in private homes, this node could have been connected and subsequently activated. Once this occurred then perhaps the nodes related to that one, let's say my views on government corruption and the Patriot Act, would have also been activated. So, even though my camera node was the one initially activated, it incidentally activated nodes assigned to other topics, thus making them more salient, or in a way, more present in my mind. This is why I stated at the beginning of this section how important it is to remember that the center node does not ever exist in a vacuum.

Ok, so to tie this into the last section about memory models, I briefly alluded to this earlier, but in an associative network model all of the nodes connected to the main one, which is the object that I am cognitively processing at the moment, contribute to my current evaluation of that object. And this is important to take note of because it highlights how our evaluations of an object, and by proxy what type of memory model we use during the cognition process, have a lot to do with our prior levels of knowledge about and our preexisting evaluations of that object, along with any other spare information that, according to our specific minds, may in some way be related. Put another way, this suggests that objects we are very familiar with will contain many strong connections to supplementary nodes because we are likely using our on-line/working memory when we are required to evaluate them. Furthermore, this means that our cognition has kept the node associated with that object activated and our evaluations of it present in our mind, which in turn has kept a stronger connection open to the related nodes. In contrast to this, though, objects we are not familiar with will likely drive us to use our long term memory, which will then lead to an associative network model that has fewer supplementary nodes, or one's with more distance between them and the main one, because long term memory contains things that we do not actively have on our mind.

To illustrate this, if I see my significant other with a lump of cash in their hand to pay a plumber for fixing our septic tank, and I am a recently recovered gambling addict who thinks about cash often, the nodes associated with gambling, consumerism, minimalism, recovery, and other related objects may be much closer to the center or even already activated in my associative network model when my "lump of cash" node is triggered. If on the other hand I am a diehard Christian and have been passively opposed to gambling my entire life, my subconscious may pay far less attention to the wad of cash and subsequently I may have an associative network model that is more sparse when it comes to supplementary nodes that I could use to make an evaluation of said cash; or in this latter scenario maybe gambling doesn't even come up because the only accessible nodes I have related to large sums of cash are a tithing node and a greed node. I digress though. Just remember that an associative network model is a system of connected nodes within our minds that we use to make evaluations, and that when one is activated others, even some that you would not assume are related, may be activated as well.

SIDENOTE

When attempting to manipulate someone (your Subject), the existence of associative network models is part of the reason establishing a baseline is so important. This is because a thorough understanding of the individual you are manipulating could help you avoid traps that you would otherwise fall into. In lay terms, based on the substance of their associative network models you can steer conversations away from nodes that are connected to things that would cause them to become agitated or suspicious. I.e., if the person you are manipulating just got cheated on while their significant other was in Vegas, be very careful bringing up gambling, casinos, and/or Nevada.

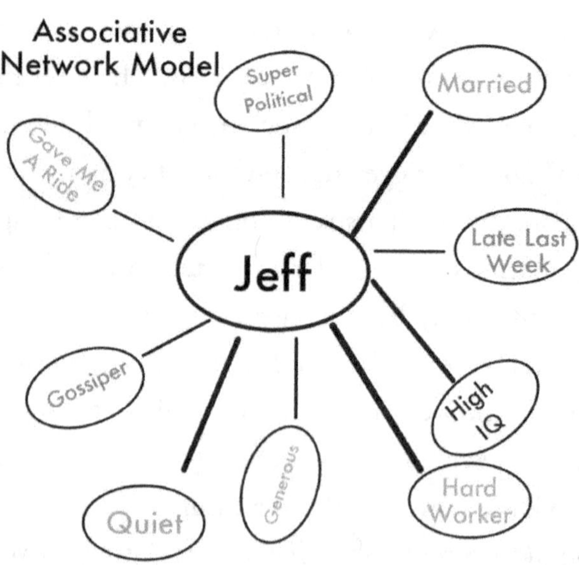

Ok, so now that you understand what an associative network model is, we have another concept to cover that will help explain why it is so important to understand which nodes are associated with which, and which ones to avoid, within your Subjects' associative network model.

If you remember a moment ago when we talked about the stages of cognition then you should remember that we also talked about how what type of memory you are using depends a lot on how much cognitive effort you are placing into evaluating an object; and also that this amount of evaluative effort, as previously discussed, affects the presence and/or strength of certain supplementary nodes in an individual's associative network model, which ultimately affects the associative network model's overall structure. Then, if you remember, our discussion of these topics led me to suggest that you want to avoid triggering any nodes that would draw unwanted attention to your manipulation and/or cause the individual you are manipulating (your Subject) to see you as a threat. Something that will help you understand this better is called **affective intelligence theory**, and in essence, affective intelligence theory states that the emotional state of an individual determines what structure of cognitive processing they will engage in. Sounds simple enough, right? Well, let's get into it then.

After carefully observing one of my former professors' extensive lectures on this topic, I began to realize that affective intelligence theory builds upon the associative network model theory because the affective intelligence theory adds two additional ways of thinking about how we, as beings who have cognition, use our levels of exposure to an object, our encoding process, and our prior memories/preexisting evaluations to make new evaluations of that object. In this way, it is like two extra layers on top of the associative network model, and the first of these layers is when our cognition uses something called our **dispositional system**.

Essentially, the dispositional system, at least in terms of cognition, is a less attentive state wherein we are relaxed and mainly using our quick-hitting on-line/working memory to evaluate the world around us. In other words, for this system imagine that you are casually strolling down a country trail. The weather is warm, but not hot, we will say it's late Spring or early Fall. The sky is clear, and you are loving the new hiking shoes you just purchased. Now in this scenario things are going well, and as a result, you are using your dispositional system of cognition because you are in a passive cognitive state. I.e., you do not have to pay very much attention to the things around you because there is nothing to be concerned and/or anxious about, and if we could see your associative network model on this leisurely stroll it would probably be full of frilly things like nature, freedom, fresh air, and the hobbies you like to do on your days off.

Now I want you to imagine that you walk up on a medium-sized rattlesnake during this casual nature walk. Immediately, unless you are a real-life version of the Crocodile Dundee, you are almost certainly going to become more alert and more anxious, right? Well, this heightened level of emotional distress you experience when you see the rattlesnake automatically activates and puts to use what is known, in affective intelligence theory, as your **surveillance system**. Put plainly, this system is the second layer of affective intelligence theory and it drives us to use more pointed and specific thought processes, which rely heavily on our LTM, because if we are in this system our subconscious mind has determined either something is not right, or that a threat is present; or put yet another way, our passive cognition has determined that it is an all hands on deck situation when it comes to how much brain power is needed. Make sense?

Anyway, in this sense you can think of this layer as a sort of defensive posture for your cognition. I.e., if you were to look at your associative network model after seeing the rattle snake, it would now likely have nodes with strong connections to venomous snakes, hospital bills, death, leaving your family, and any number of other nodes that are related to something inherently negative.

This change in what type of cognitive structure and subsequent memory storage method you are using can happen in an instant and is just another reason to take baselines seriously. This is because the surveillance system can be activated by many different things depending on the specific person you are manipulating, and once activated it can have a lasting effect. For instance, in this case if you were to make it out of the woods and you were not prepared to or even concerned with seeing a snake before you went in, this lack of mental preparation would have made the snake something you were not familiar with. The surprise of it, therefore, would have a very strong impact on your cognition and may even lead to the formation of a negative node in your associative network model connected strongly to the hiking node, which would influence your evaluations of hiking the next time you were thinking about going. Good to go?

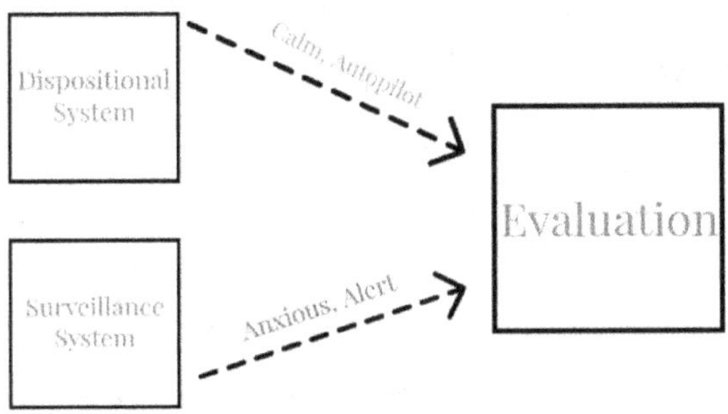

To give a more practical example, as far as this book is concerned anyway, imagine that you are trying to manipulate your boss into giving you a promotion and because you are somewhat unknown around the office you need him to first notice you, and then to feel somewhat favorable toward you, for this to happen. And the reason you want to approach it this way is because when he interacts with you in the future, or even just sees your name on a list of potential employees to promote, you want to make sure the node for you in his associative network model is strongly associated with positive memories and/or things like hard work, dedication, and client management skills. Now to do this you decide you are going to bring him a novel proposal on Friday because, well, who isn't in a better mood when they are about to get off work for the weekend, regarding a project that would be good for the company, and by proxy, him.

During the lead up to this day, things are going fairly well. You get your work done early enough to work on the proposal, you make sure he doesn't see you in the break room chit-chatting, only at your desk working hard, and you even make casual conversation with him in the elevator about his favorite sports team, which is a team from an opposing city and something that your coworkers would likely not have assumed and/or used during their own conversations with the boss. In other words, everything is set and he has been primed perfectly for the friction point of your manipulation.

On Friday you are trembling with excitement and adrenaline, but nonetheless you suppress these feelings, walk into his office, say "Sir, could I have a moment?" and then lay it on him. To your surprise, he tells you, not angrily, but sternly that the proposal isn't solid and to get out of his office. Perplexed, you walk out with your proposal for a company-sponsored animal shelter in hand, which was something you had worked very hard on mind you, and ask yourself, what went wrong? I mean, you established a solid baseline, laid the groundwork, and even made sure to wait until the specific day that he was most likely to be stress-free and in his dispositional system. The failure boggles your mind and confuses you.

Well, what you hadn't paid attention to during your baseline analysis was that the boss had just put down his long-time pet. Now you would have taken note of this if you had noticed he was unusually short as of late, hadn't come into work with his pet at all that week, something that generally happens at least twice every work week, and also that he has a new photo of him and his pet on his desk with a small "In Memoria" quote at the bottom. But you didn't and by missing these cues you have instead accidentally put yourself into a situation wherein you activated your boss's surveillance system, thus causing his cognition to associate your node with the loss of his recent pet. Make sense? You see, even though your proposal is technically unrelated to his pet, and is actually something he normally would love, it is still connected enough to that pet node that it, essentially, changed how his cognition was processing information, which, rather obviously made him less likely to view your information as favorable.

Ok, now that you have a basic understanding of how affective intelligence theory builds on the associative network model theory, I want to move on and get into some specific considerations for each one of the structures of cognition, or more specifically, things that people trying to manipulate someone else's cognition should take into consideration; but first I need to talk about some barriers to effective cognition that could be both a blessing and a curse for people engaging in a manipulation like the one mentioned above.

The first barrier to proper cognition, which we essentially just covered so I'll keep it brief, is emotions. To elaborate, as stated before, a heightened state of emotional distress can cause our surveillance system to engage, and this is obviously a bad occurrence if you are trying to manipulate someone. The reason, well, put plainly, when a person's surveillance system is engaged this means that they are hyper-aware of and focused on their surroundings. But distress is not the only emotion that affects our cognition. In a much broader context, increased overall levels of emotion, even positive ones, still have an effect on our cognitive evaluations because increased levels of emotion put us into one of the two states of emotional cognition. Now this state of emotional cognition is known as hot cognition and it is something you need to know about; but before I explain what this type of emotional cognition is (heightened emotions), I want to first explain what the other state is.

To begin, the first type of emotional cognition, which is called **cold cognition**, is basically where our cognitive processes, ironically, are operating emotion-free. This is to say that while in a state of cold cognition our evaluations are not influenced by emotion, but rather by logical thought. Now, even though the degree of exposure we have to an object, as well as our memories and/or prior evaluations of that object all factor in like normal during cold cognition, which could significantly impact our success or failure mind you, nonetheless, while a Subject is in this state they are far less likely to be irrational. Ergo, it is generally preferable for manipulators to keep their subjects using cold cognition, and not hot cognition.

Now the second state of emotional cognition, on the other hand, is called **hot cognition**, and this is when we are cognitively processing an object while also experiencing a heightened level of emotions, positive or negative. To think of this state, I think about a person who is angry at someone else saying to that person, "You are getting me heated!" You see, this person is likely not going to be thinking clearly because, as well all know, angry people do unpredictable and sometimes irrational things. Not too good for someone who is relying heavily on using a baseline analysis to choose a course of action when it comes to manipulation, aye? At any rate, this example of an angry person goes well with the term hot cognition and makes it easy to understand, but you should know that this state also includes positive emotions. In other words, hot cognition is when our emotions are actively impacting our cognitive processes, even if they are emotions that make us happy.

To picture this in real world terms, think about how people behave when talking about the weather vs sports, politics, and/or religion. As you no doubt already know, in the latter scenarios people are a lot more likely to behave irrationally, whether it is overly cheerful after their team wins, or overly glum when their political candidate loses, because these are all things that people take personally and feel very strongly about. Make sense? Good, because this emotional connection to objects is what drives us to a state of hot cognition, and when we are in this state, we are much more unpredictable, and therefore much more difficult to manipulate; unless, of course, this is actually part of your plan and you are guiding their emotional reactions in a way that benefits you (which can be done). But, even then, this is a delicate tightrope walk and has a lot of potential for failure, so my advice is to try and keep your Subject out of hot cognition at all costs. I.e., avoid topics that they feel overly passionate about.

Ok, one last thing to consider in regard to hot and cold cognition is that these two states of emotional arousal, at least in the context of cognitive processing, do not exist in a vacuum. This is to say that, like the two types of memory, both can be used at the same time like a Venn diagram wherein each overlap slightly (I.e., no one is ever 100% emotion free, nor 100% emotional). However, like memory one state will always be dominant, and therefore you should account for which of these two states your Subject is more likely to be in when you are planning to manipulate that individual. Especially because people often overlook and/or do not consider overly positive emotions to be a part of the surveillance system, which, in a way, they still are. Anyway, to that end, and as a final note on this topic, be careful not to get the Subject of your manipulation overly excited with positive emotions because this can, like an angry Subject, still make them irrational and their behavior hard to predict.

Alright, moving on from emotion, in the next chapter we are going to talk about the academic models of persuasion, but to foreshadow that a bit, a major implication in the way we perceive messages depends upon how much we are paying attention to them. This is to say that most people in first-world countries are pretty lazy when it comes to their cognitive processing. That, or maybe they are just too busy bringing home the proverbial bacon and dealing with your shitty in-laws to expend precious cognitive resources on secondary and tertiary things existing in the world around them. Either way, because we have a lot of information to process on a day-to-day basis and often not a lot of desire and/or ability to do so, we generally need little mental cheat sheets to help us make evaluations along the way. These cheat sheets are called **heuristics**.

Heuristics, in essence, are cognitive shortcuts based on our prior evaluations/memories that we use when we need to make a decision fast, and either can't or don't want to expend a lot of mental energy, and politics is the perfect tool we can use to explain how we use these shortcuts. To illustrate, Philip E. Converse, in 1964, published an academic masterpiece, as far as I am concerned anyway, called *The Nature of Belief Systems in Mass Publics*. In this work, Converse essentially aimed to figure out how different types of people felt at the time about specific issues in the realm of politics; and after his exhaustive work he found some interesting answers that, as a Libertarian leaning fella, give me both hope and dread for the political future of our country. I digress though. His results can be summed up beautifully in this quote, which he used to end the peer-reviewed work.

> *"The broad contours of elite decisions over time can depend in a vital way upon currents in what is loosely called "the history of ideas." These decisions in turn have effects upon the mass of more common citizens. But, of any direct participation in this history of ideas and the behavior it shapes, the mass is remarkably innocent. We do not disclaim the existence of entities that might best be called "folk ideologies," nor do we deny for a moment that strong differentiations in a variety of narrower values may be found within subcultures of less educated people. Yet for the familiar belief systems that, in view of their historical importance, tend most to attract the sophisticated observer, it is likely that an adequate mapping of a society (or, for that matter, the world) would provide a jumbled cluster of pyramids or a mountain range, with sharp delineation and differentiation in beliefs from elite apex to elite apex but with the mass bases of the pyramids overlapping in such profusion that it would be impossible to decide where one pyramid ended and another began."*

Essentially, what this quote is saying is that the political elites, such as politicians, prominent public commentators, and wealthy individuals in the donor class, for the most part all strictly adhere to an existing political ideology. In other words, when polled about fictional scenarios, wherein no political parties were identified, conservative elites almost always agreed with the conservative stance on each individual issue, and liberal elites almost always agreed with the liberal one. However, this consistent adherence to a specific ideology is not something that existed when he looked at the average person. Pretty wild, right?

You see, according to Converse's study most of us average Joes are all over the place when it comes to what stances we do or do not take on specific issues; however, nearly everyone in this country who votes identifies as either a Republican or a Democrat. And furthermore, when polled about the same issues, and this time made aware of what party supports which issue, the mass public snapped into shape and, like the elites, voted nearly in line or completely in line with "their teams" ideology. Case in point, even though most people don't actually agree with everything their political "team" believes in, when asked to make political evaluations they almost always defer to that "team," if that information is available. Why, you ask? The answer is simple, heuristics. I.e., I don't have to think about which position I think is best, I know what my party thinks, so I will just take the shortcut and pick their side.

SIDENOTE

An interesting aspect of Converse's data is the part where it covers how the elites influence the formation of ideological groups and identities. I say this because if the elites adhere to the tenants of their partisan identity (political affiliation) even when they don't know which position is which teams, but the mass public does not do this, then we can assume that the elites feel more strongly about and are more dedicated to their chosen ideologies. In other words, the elites "truly" believe what they believe, and the masses, more often than not, are just playing follow the leader.

Because the results were so conclusive regarding the differences between elite and average voters, at least when it comes to issue-specific evaluations, it stands to reason that the elites form, or at the very least, propagate ideologies, not the masses (The elites are the ones who drive the belief systems.). As Converse points out, if the inverse were true and the masses were actually the source of power behind the development of ideologies and ideological groups, well, then we would see clearly defined groups in the masses' survey results, not the overlapping pyramid bases Converse actually found. Anyway, this, when combined with supplementary political psychology research that suggests individuals mostly get their beliefs from elite influence leads me to the belief that elites form ideologies, dedicate themselves to those ideologies, and then many of us, as I suggested above, just play follow the leader. Now this may be difficult to think about, but the data does suggest this, or at the very least that most average citizens do not vote the way that they truly feel, which gives us something to think about. I.e., does this mean that the elites are manipulating us to think or act in certain ways? Perhaps that is something you should think about next time you are asked about a controversial issue.... Any who, back to the topic at hand.

What Converse's research tells me is that most people do not expend a lot of cognitive energy when they vote. Why is this you ask? The answer, as I said above, is heuristics. You see, when I am at a dinner party and someone asks me about healthcare reform it is far easier to simply see what my political leaders say about healthcare reform and parrot that than it is to go out and do a lot of independent research, come up with a neutral position that takes the best from both sides, and then share that evaluation with people who may find it unpopular. No, that second option is much too complicated. Ergo, a better solution, at least for most of us, is to activate the healthcare reform node in our mind and then see what political nodes are attached (For Republicans, these nodes would likely be negative, but the inverse would likely be true for Democrats.).

SIDENOTE

Reminder! Social status can be different depending on the culture or subculture an individual exists in.

Continuing on with this topic, heuristics can be both useful and dangerous when it comes to manipulation. This is because heuristics are an aspect of cognition that relies heavily on our LTM and on-line/ working memories, as well as our previously made evaluations. For instance, if I know that a girl that I want to go out with is going to use heuristics when it comes to choosing whom to date, which is perfectly natural and something that we all do, I may try putting on a nice watch or, depending on the girl, carrying my motorcycle helmet with me before I go talk to her. The idea behind this is that she will see these cues and be more likely to infer things about me that raise my social status within her associative network model. I.e., the watch indicates that I am financially loaded and the motorcycle helmet indicates I am a bit of a bad boy. But this can also go the other way as well. In other words, if the girl I want to ask out has a thing for money and instead of approaching her with a nice watch on I decide ask her out in front of my beat-up 2013 Ford Focus while wearing a holy t-shirt, the likely result is that she will immediately use heuristics to determine that I do not have money, style, or, frankly, enough game to know not to highlight my crappy car when asking a beautiful woman out, and therefore am a man undeserving of her attention. Get it?

Given the prevalence of heuristic use in the average person's cognitive processing (how often we use them), it is very important to understand what heuristics we are driving the Subject of our manipulation to use. I.e., just like water follows the path of least resistance, unless we can drive them to think and make evaluations while using the central route of persuasion, which involves higher levels of cognitive reasoning and is something that we will talk about in the next chapter, people's minds will almost always take the shortcut and use heuristics. In fact, after my research I would say that this is the case nine times out of ten. So, pay attention to them.

Ok, next topic. The final barrier to proper cognition that I want to touch on is called **motivated reasoning**. To begin, anyone who watches and/or reads political content likely knows the term motivated reasoning, but the truth is that very few people actually understand it. In lay terms, motivated reasoning is when someone's cognition is clouded by an objective that is secondary to making an accurate evaluation, and this secondary motivation is, basically, to win the communicative interaction, which again is just a manipulative dance, at all costs. Now it is worth noting that motivated reasoning, as you no doubt noticed, can look a lot like hot cognition, so it is important to know the difference.

Though the two can be and often times are very similar, motivated reasoning is different than an inaccurate evaluation that was induced by hot cognition in that during motivated reasoning the individual's cognition is working towards a specific goal from the beginning. In other words, the person communicating is doing so with their mind already made up. To illustrate, an example of hot cognition clouding someone's mind would be an individual getting emotional over a good faith but heated religious debate and failing to understand the points that the other individual was making. I.e., imagine a Muslim getting angry at an atheist for not believing in the existence of God and stating in a heated tone that there is a God and that the atheist is just arrogant and deceived, despite the atheist making a more logically sound argument. Put simply, this is an example of clouded thinking due to hot cognition. Put another way, the Muslim went into the debate with an open mind, but simply got heated, and subsequently stubborn when they started to lose.

If instead, however, motivated reasoning was being used, the Muslims argument might more closely resemble something along the lines of him calmly stating "You say there is no proof of God, but there is proof all around you." Now what is the difference, you ask? Well, the difference in this second example is that in that scenario either a conscious or subconscious portion of the Muslims cognition is actively arguing to prove the existence of God, despite the other persons argument, and because of this they have made an illogical argument by imposing a causal relationship between two things (God and everything around them) and ignoring all of the other possibilities (Evolution, simulation theory, etc.), which they would have done in an honest and open minded debate. In other words, even if the Muslim thought he was approaching the debate with an open mind, in reality he came in with an objective, proving that God is real, and never stood a chance of seeing things from the atheist's point of view.

This is why motivated reasoning can be difficult to deal with. You see, in the atheist vs Muslim scenario illustrated above, no number of logical arguments will sway the Muslim because their cognition is actively screening out and, essentially, refusing to process the threatening information brought forth by the atheist, regardless of whether it has merit or not; and this can be dangerous in manipulation because when you are manipulating a Subject you may hit a topic that makes the Subject irrational and/or illogically unmovable (Politics and religion are often topics that drive people to use motivated reasoning.).

Now since it is impossible to avoid someone's motivated reasoning entirely, in these situations wherein their cognition is firmly dug in, assuming you mistakenly stumbled into it and did not intentionally set it up that is (something you can do, but it is still risky), it may be best to form a new strategy as opposed to pushing the envelope. And the reason for this is that it is nearly impossible to alter someone's evaluations of a topic once they are engaging in motivated reasoning.

Of course, this is also not a hard and fast rule, just a piece of friendly advice. This is to say that there is another side of this coin that can be used. In other words, it is extremely risky, but sometimes it is actually a smart strategy to use a Subject's motivated reasoning against them. For example, if you think you could pull it off, you could feign an offensive debate even while knowing that the Subject will engage in motivated reasoning.

To illustrate, after a good intellectual fight, which shows you as a cognitive force that warrants mutual respect, you can feign defeat, thus making the opponent feel like they are mentally superior to you and that, even though you deserve respect, you are not a threat. This, again, is important for manipulation and keeping the Subject in their dispositional system, which will be even more important when we get to the archetypes of power chapter, because it gives them the illusion of power over you. But like I said, live by motivated reasoning die by motivated reasoning. I.e., they could gain respect for you while also feeling as if they dominated you, or alternatively they could decide that you are a cunt and subsequently set their sights on making your life miserable. Capeesh?

Alright, as a final note on this topic, remember that motivated reasoning can happen consciously, which would be what I would call a bad faith argument, or subconsciously, which more closely resembles cognitive dissonance. Take note of which is being used by evaluating the depth of the individual's prior knowledge on the topic and also evaluating if they use personal ad hominem attacks to beat your position. The former (high levels of knowledge about the topic) is indicative of subconscious motivated reasoning and is something you can work with. In lay terms, this means that they are not aware that their cognition is clouded and they are simply trying to honestly win, even if their subconscious is not. But the latter (Ad Hominem/personal attacks), on the other hand, means that you are probably dealing with the conscious version of motivated reasoning, and also a bad-faith actor. In these bad-faith scenarios proceed with caution because bad faith actors are far more naturally talented when it comes to sousing out manipulation (It takes one to know one I guess!) and they are also aware that they are being intellectually dishonest (Thus why they have to use calm personal attacks in lieu of logic and facts. AKA, they don't even belief what they are saying.), which means their behavior could be highly irrational and/or unpredictable. Good to go?

All right, we are finally at the end of this chapter folks. I know it may have been a bit less interesting for some of you, but as you will see in the next chapter understanding how our brains process, store, and use information is very important. Furthermore, when it comes to the individual dimensions of lies, and specific manipulation strategies, being aware of how different emotional states and/or other cognitive barriers factor into the process is a crucial part of planning your manipulations and making them successful. Now, with that said, I just want to briefly end this chapter with a few specific considerations for each stage of the cognition process, at least in regard to manipulation, because I know that some of this information was dense and may have been hard to understand. Those considerations are as follows:

Exposure—When you are attempting to manipulate someone's perceived reality it is important that you, for lack of a better phrase, control the narrative because as we just learned, the individual you are focused on has an associative network model, wherein they will associate one object with multiple memories and/or preexisting evaluations. So make sure you guide the conversation toward the nodes you want activated, and away from those you don't. Also, as we just learned there are two systems our body uses for emotional cognitive processing, the dispositional system, and the surveillance system. When manipulating someone you want to be very careful that you have established an accurate baseline for them because this will allow you to expose them to only things that activate the nodes, and subsequent system of emotional cognition that you want. I.e., in a work setting, because this book is after all called "How To Get Out Of Work," when it comes to the Subject making personal evaluations of *you* it is best to keep your Subject in a dispositional state while also reinforcing your image positively in their associative network model.

Of course, with this said, the surveillance system, as well as negative nodes, can be used to your advantage in certain situations as well. For instance, if you wanted to, say, get a competitive promotion at work, you could activate a node in your boss's associative network model that is connected to one of your coworkers in a negative way. I.e., perhaps a female coworker of yours is a party gal on the weekends and your boss just got cheated on by his wife while she was at the club. Well, what you could do in this situation is mention the fact, on a Monday when he asks about your weekend, that it was slow, but that you were also tempted to go out with your coworker because "they like to get wild on the weekends." You see, by doing this you have associated your coworker's node with a party node inside of your boss's associative network model, through manipulating the exposure stage of his cognition, which could be connected in a number of ways to the boss's cheating wife. Ergo, this will activate his surveillance system, but the focus will be on your coworker, not you. But just don't forget that, regardless of the individual situation, object nodes in an associative network model do not exist in a vacuum and will always be cross referenced with other object nodes, with the result being that sometimes unrelated nodes get triggered by accident. So be careful!

Encoding—Because you want the individual you are manipulating to only associate you with the nodes you choose, it is important to control the amount of information their cognition has to encode you. This will drive them to be more thoughtful in their evaluations of you when the time comes and will also limit the number of heuristics they have available in the meantime to make snap judgements about you, which could be negative. To explain, you can think about this as being invisible in the open. I.e., do far more listening than talking and try to steer conversations away from anything deep or meaningful, unless, of course, these topics are necessary to your manipulation, such as making a strong case for a political candidate only to let your opponent win because you want to use motivated reasoning and/or feigning defeat as a technique. In this situation, yes, you have given them a heuristic to use in regard to you, your political affiliation, but you have also given their cognition the ability to view you through their dispositional system, and not as a threat that requires deeper surveillance. In sum, you only want the Subject of your manipulation to know what you want them to know about you, so control access to the information they have available to encode.

Evaluations—Always remember that, depending on whether the Subject of your manipulation is using their LTM or on-line/working memory, your Subjects' evaluations are not permanent. So, be mindful of negative interactions or events that could change them prior to the friction point of your manipulation, such as a pet dying, for instance. Also, in the evaluation stage avoid accidentally activating their surveillance system and/or driving them to use hot cognition. The reason, though a useful tool in some circumstances, hot cognition often makes subjects irrational, thus making it difficult to predict their behavior.

In addition to this, keep in mind that some evaluations may be influenced by motivated reasoning. If this is the case, be it because of a consciously bad actor or its more sincere counterpart, subconscious motivated reasoning, it is still unlikely you will succeed with any sort of persuasion technique if the Subject is using motivated reasoning and you are not prepared for it. Ergo, my advice when it comes to the evaluation stage and counteracting motivated reasoning is to regularly drive your Subject to update their evaluations of you in a positive way. This reinforces the connections of your node to positive nodes in their associative network model, and also gives them positive heuristics to use when encoding/evaluating anything you are involved in.

And just as a parting word of caution when it comes to evaluations, be careful when influencing someone to make negative evaluations of another object. Put another way, you do not want them to label you as a gossiper, untrustworthy, and/or unprofessional. So, do not be overt and instead lead them to make these evaluations indirectly, just like the party gal example. Now, this strategy may seem like it is too subtle, but remember, just like outrunning a bear, you do not have to beat down the other person you are competing with, you just have to outrun them, which you can do by focusing on improving the Subjects' evaluations of you more than focusing on cutting down your enemies.

Storage—If you handle all of the other three stages correctly, storage should not be a stage you are heavily concerned with. This is because, assuming you *have* handled them correctly, whether or not the Subject is using LTM or on-line/working memory to make evaluations of you, or an object you are using, they will have positive and strongly reinforced node connections, memories, and preexisting evaluations available and ready to use. So, yeah, you should not be overly concerned with storage unless you fucked up somewhere down the line and need to reset the narrative.

To give you an example, if your plan to highlight your coworkers' party lifestyle backfires because the boss is actually in a post-divorce party phase themselves (and therefore likes the idea of a party gal), you will want to undo the association you placed in his mind that makes you seem prudish or bland, and this will require getting around the heuristics you led him to use for you and guiding him to take another, more thoughtful look. This is to say that perhaps you place a picture of you at a music festival on your desk; and the music festival, by the way, so long as it does not show any specific concert details regarding who performed, "could" happen to have been one that featured an artist you know the boss likes. I digress though.

When the boss asks about your weekend, or even inquires about the photo, you now have an opportunity to discuss how you are deciding to live for yourself again and that you are done moping around feeling bad about your breakup. Furthermore, you could even tell them that you are forcing yourself out of your shell and that you are going to have a wild phase, because you have earned it. In sum, if the conversation is stimulating to the boss, which the specific artist you chose to introduce can help with, then you can make them focus specifically on you enough to reevaluate you, thus changing your status in their associative network model, LTM, and on-line memory simultaneously from a prude to a party boy, with the result being that you replaced the old heuristics, boring and bland, with ones that are more useful to your goals of earning their favor.

Well, that is it everyone. I hope you did actually end up enjoying the chapter, even if it was a bit drier than the others, but either way I will see you in the next chapter wherein we will be discussing the academic models of persuasion, and even a little bit about the relationship between attitudes and behavior, both of which, as a nerd, I think are quite sexy.

What is Persuasion

Thus rhetoric, it seems, is a producer of persuasion for belief, not instruction in the matter of right and wrong...And so the rhetorician's business is not to instruct a law court or a public meeting in matters of right and wrong, but only to make them believe. —**Plato**

Well, we are finally here folks. The beginning of the sexy part of the book is upon us and I don't know about you, but I am excited. This is to say that, even though I did find the first half of the book enjoyable to research and write, this chapter, as well as the rest of the book, gets into the actual meat and potatoes of the manipulation process, as well as my unique contributions to this field of study. Now with that said, again, this second half of the book, like the first, isn't some secret codex that will make you irresistible to women, or an overnight millionaire, but what it will do is detail and outline part of a framework that teaches you how to manipulate perceived reality and practically apply what we have learned so far. Good to go?

Now, because I feel like you have had enough introductions that explain why each individual chapter exists, I will skip that format for this one. Plus, I mean, this chapter is specifically about persuasion, so, if you have read and/or listened all the way up until this point it will kind of be obvious why this chapter was included. Well, dammit. There I go again turning an introduction that is not meant to be a lengthy introduction, ironically, into a lengthy introduction. You know what, I am going to nip this in the bud. Blah blah blah let's get into it.

Ok, so now that we know what cognition is and roughly how all of its many facets work together to make evaluations of the world around us, I want to move on and discuss how these evaluations can be manipulated through the process of persuasion. More specifically, I want to talk about how to use persuasion, which is ultimately just changing what people think (their attitudes) and what they do (their behaviors), to make people act in a way that you desire. Now here at the outset, let me just say that the reason I use the terms attitudes *and* behaviors is because there is still a lot of disagreement in the academic community about whether attitudes influence behaviors, or behaviors influence attitudes; but nonetheless these are the two variables that persuasion aims to change. Make sense? Good. For time's sake I'll save you the trouble of going through all of the studies focused on this debate by telling you here first that there actually isn't one single right answer to this question (A full reference list for these studies, as well as all of the other studies used in this chapter is at the end of the book. Even though I just saved you some time, I would still highly advise giving them a look.).

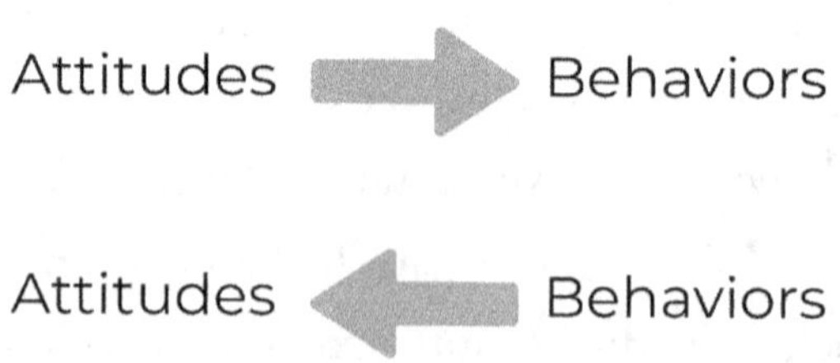

To elaborate, when it comes to attitudes and behavior, much like how I believe in a hybrid-style model of memory storage, I think that the research and evidence both support the idea that these factors influence one another in significant ways. What I mean by this is that at times our attitudes about something, we will use the political landscape here, can lead us to engage in certain behaviors. I.e., let's say my friends begin to discuss politics regularly with me and I become very interested in and passionate about politics as a result of wanting to fit in. In this instance, maybe the way that these newly formed attitudes impact my behavior entails voting or even going to a political rally for the first time. Makes sense, right?

On the other hand, often times our behaviors may actually be the thing that influences our attitudes, not the other way around. An example of this would be you becoming a political junkie after going to a political rally because you want to be a part of a new group of friends, who all happen to be super into politics. In other words, let's assume that you do not particularly care about the political landscape and you do not discuss it regularly, but you do want to fit in with this new group of politics junkies because it will be beneficial for networking and your future career. Well, if you keep attending political rallies with these friends, so that you can keep associating yourself more and more with this specific group, according to something called **self-presentation theory**, which essentially just means that you become whom you pretend to be (This is also where the term dress for the job you want not the job you have comes from.), you will eventually start to see yourself as a political person. And this new self-image, which will lead to a change in your attitude about politics, may then lead to you engaging in even more behaviors that are centered around politics, such as volunteering for a campaign, going door-to-door to collect petition signatures, or even running for office because our self-image is often a major factor in the process of decision-making. Ergo, when it is all said and done, the behavior of engaging with politics actually caused your attitude to change about politics, not the other way around, which in turn led you to engage in yet even more political activity.

As you can see, we have a real chicken and egg conundrum with the ole attitudes and behaviors debate, but once again I do not like the need of many academics to put things into one of several neat and all-encompassing pre-formed boxes. So, I say to accept both theories because both theories, attitudes shaping behaviors and behaviors shaping attitudes, have something to offer manipulators. I.e., if your goal is to persuade someone's attitude about an object, with the end goal being to change their behavior, you could use a technique like the **mere exposure effect**, which is essentially when an you use an overwhelming amount of exposure to something unfavorable to alter your Subjects' preexisting evaluations of that thing, with the goal being to change their behavior toward that object. For instance, how many songs have you hated at first only to end up loving them after the hundredth time, and then how many of those did you end up playing constantly for years to come? You see, this is a perfect illustration of how the mere exposure effect works to alter our attitudes, and then our behaviors.

Now, even though this is a relatively simple example, it nonetheless shows very clearly how an attitude change (liking the song) can change our behavior (playing that song for years to come). However, if instead your goal is to specifically manipulate someone's attitude through altering their behavior, perhaps you want them to want to buy something from you let's say, then you could use what is called the **foot-in-the-door technique**, which is when you get an individual to make a small commitment before eventually asking them for a larger commitment. Using the sales scenario again, you would do this by first getting the Subject to agree to only try out the item for a free trial period. Then, once the individual has committed to trying the new item and is now using it (behavior change), according to the foot-in-the-door technique it is also likely that their self-image will change to reflect someone who would own and use the product you are selling (attitude change). Ergo, they will likely purchase that item.

In this second scenario, as you can see, by getting the individual to engage in a certain behavior you subsequently altered their attitude about the product, which will, in all likelihood, change their future behavior. And just for your information, if you didn't know this already, this is the real reason that clothing stores let you try on items before buying them. In other words, it is not because they want you to see if the items fit. No, instead marketing experts realized that after potential customers saw themselves in the items they were thinking about purchasing, they became much more likely to pull the proverbial trigger. Thus, they decided to set up a system that incentivizes behaviors that alter attitudes.

SIDENOTE

As I said before in chapter one, this book provides a unique look at the individual parts of the manipulation process as a whole, as well as a framework for my contribution to this research and the four types of lies. I tried to provide as many practical real world examples as possible, but for things like specific persuasion techniques (i.e., the mere exposure effect and the foot in the door technique) there is just not enough room in this book to cover all of them. Luckily, if all of this stuff interests you then you can look further into all of the works referenced in these pages, as well as the actual references section I include at the end. But in addition to these sources, you can also find endless academic articles on all of the subjects discussed in this book by simply using Google Scholar or JSTOR, which are free databases full of academic studies. Now I bring this up because I do have to warn you that there is a lot of bullshit out there when you leave the academic community, especially when it comes to manipulation. This is to say that there are a million and one pseudo-science books and online subscription services that claim to give you the perfect thing to say to get laid or the perfect business strategy to get rich. Well, as you have seen so far, there is no one size fits all solution when it comes to manipulation because humans are just too unpredictable, irrational, and unique. So, yes, I would cross reference any specific techniques you find against the foundational elements and manipulation framework contained in this book because, even though some of them can actually be useful, I still believe that you will have far better success if you instead understand the foundational elements of manipulation and then use those to approach each situation differently. In any case, with that said still feel free to check out some of this "How To" material because, if nothing else, this book will allow you to see any potential weak points in those 3rd party techniques, which you can then prepare for accordingly, while also allowing you to use the substantive parts of them that pair well with your specific manipulation.

Alright, so now that you know a little bit about how attitudes and behaviors impact one another, I will leave it up to you which one you want to target with your particular manipulation. This is because at the end of the day the academic models of persuasion are the same for each, regardless of which you are targeting. Anyway, speaking of the academic models of persuasion there are three specific models that I want to cover and I don't see any reason to keep beating around the proverbial bush. So, let's get into it.

The first academic model of persuasion, which was created by Dr. Petty and Dr. Cacioppo in 1981, is called **The Elaboration Likelihood Model (ELM)**. In essence, this model is comprised of two primary elements, and as the name would suggest, the first of these is elaboration. Within the context of the ELM, elaboration refers to the extent to which an individual can or wants to think about an object. So, when it comes to the topic of politics, for instance, elaboration would refer to how much time a person *can* spend thinking about politics and their overall levels of motivation to do so. I.e., an individual who is either uninterested in politics or doesn't have the time to keep up with them will have very low levels of elaboration when it comes to political issues; however, a political junkie like me who works in that field, on the other hand, will have rather high levels of elaboration when it comes to those same topics. Make sense?

The second element of the elaboration likelihood model (ELM), again, as the name suggests, is likelihood, and this is, basically, the likelihood that an individual will actually spend time thinking about an object. Now it is worth noting that external factors, such as where you live and what information you have access to can and do have a major impact on the likelihood metric. I.e., an individual who works in the tech field and is a regular reader of the Wall Street Journal is very likely to have a lot of ability when it comes to seeking out political information. Thus, the chance of them doing so is far greater than someone living as a lumberjack in the middle of the woods with no internet, even if both possess the same motivation to study politics. The reason, as you probably surmised, is that the second individual simply does not have access to that information. Simple enough, right?

SIDENOTE

As you can see, the levels of elaboration (how much the person can/is thinking about the object) has a direct connection with the likelihood metric. I.e., if a person wants to elaborate on politics, but does not have internet and/or other forms of obtaining political information, it is not very likely that they will actually end up thinking about that topic very much.

What we see forming when we observe the elaboration likelihood model is a very clear relationship between motivation and ability. Now I bring that up because this leads us to the elaboration likelihood models two routes of persuasion; or in other words, how this model is actually used. To begin, the first route is called the central route, and this route of persuasion is, put plainly, when the receiver, or individual being persuaded, uses thoughtful and careful consideration of the information present and/or available to their cognition to make an evaluation. In lay terms, it is when an individual is both motivated to pay attention to something (high elaboration) and also has the ability to do so (high likelihood).

To illustrate, if I was to ask you what you thought about one of our mutual friends' relationships with the hidden purpose of ultimately convincing you not to like their significant other; if you genuinely cared about our friends' relationship and had plenty of access to the intricate details of it, you would most likely use logical and reasonable cognitive processes (The Central Route) to make a thorough and detailed evaluation of their relationship. This is because, again, you have both the ability to think deeply about their relationship, and also lots of motivation to do so. Ergo, when asked it is very likely you will spend a lot of cognitive energy thinking about it.

Now when manipulating you in this scenario, since I know that you will use central processing to formulate an attitude (opinion) about our friends' relationship, I would make sure that the message of my manipulation was not emotional, but instead very fact-based and logical. This is to say that perhaps I would use a simple pro/con list that I have weighted in the direction I want (more cons than pros); or, alternatively, perhaps I will make reasonable claims about the friend's significant other not being respectful of the relationship. The reason, because you will be spending a lot of cognitive effort evaluating my persuasive case, I want to make sure my argument isn't shallow and/or surface level (Don't worry, this will make more sense when you see the illustration.).

Alright, so continuing on with this subject, the central route can be somewhat of a barrier to manipulators in that it means the Subject is highly attentive to whatever you are discussing and less likely to use things like heuristics. This is why, in general, I try to avoid using the central route (if possible) and instead try to structure my manipulations so that the Subject is not very focused on what I am doing. This, I have found, leads to less resistance on their part, and therefore, higher overall levels of success. All that considered, though, you should still not sleep on this route because it can also, in certain circumstances, be critical to have this tool in your manipulative toolbox. For example, remember the rewiring strategy regarding your boss and partying that I mentioned in the last chapter? Do you also remember that after that individual flubbed the manipulation by miscalculating the boss's baseline behavior (he incorrectly wanted the boss to see him as a prude), he needed the boss to take a closer look at him because, otherwise, he would have come across as unfavorable when the boss compared them to the fun party gal in the office? Well, by drawing the boss in with the picture, stimulating conversation, and mutual interests the employee was forcing the boss to slow down and use the central route of cognition to reevaluate their attitude towards said employee. In other words, instead of influencing the boss's attitude through subtle peripheral cues, the employee made them stop and really invest some cognitive energy into thinking about them until they changed their mind. Make sense? Good, because this is exactly the type of scenario that would require the use of the central route of persuasion and a reminder that, as long as you do your best to avoid activating their surveillance system unnecessarily, the elaboration likelihood model's central route of persuasion can be a very useful manipulative concept.

SIDENOTE

The main purpose of the ELM is to help you understand how your Subject is processing information. I.e., it lets you, the manipulator, know whether you need to focus on surface level shit, or logic when manipulating them.

Ok, so that is the central route of persuasion, but there is another half of this model that is just as important. This is to say that, on the other end of the elaboration-likelihood continuum lies the opposite route of the central one. This route is called the peripheral route and, in essence, it is one that involves either low *motivation* to spend cognitive resources (low elaboration), low *ability* to expend cognitive resources (low likelihood), or both.

Essentially, this route is when an individual uses shallow cues and/or shortcuts, like heuristics, to form evaluations about an object, and when using the peripheral route it is crucial to keep the Subject in their dispositional system so that you can use that route to lead them where you want them to go without any serious thought or consideration on their part. Put another way, if they do remain in this dispositional state, you, as the manipulator, can guide them using cues that induce attitude/behavior changes without necessitating scrutiny in regard to the argument itself.

To illustrate this, let's use the example from the last chapter about the boss who had recently lost their pet. If you were to do that situation over using the peripheral route of persuasion you would want to avoid bringing the topic of pets up in the first place because it would activate their surveillance system and/or hot cognition, thus causing them to use central route processing, by immediately reminding them of their dog and making them "care" more about your proposal. So, instead, you may be better off trying an approach that evokes positive emotions, but also only mild levels of interest from your boss. Now to do this while avoiding having to completely redo your proposal, you would want to change that proposals focus; or at the very least what he sees highlighted in your proposal, which was previously the animal aspect, to instead the financial gains this proposed plan would provide for the company. I.e., you could change your presentation of the proposal so that now you discuss a conservation-style plan that is going to be popular among young people, thus increasing the company's social equity (The animals are secondary and simply a means of getting young people, the real target, more involved with your company.). Hell, you could even, if it were a video-style presentation, use inspirational music as a tool to elicit positive emotions from the boss without even having to go into too much detail on the actual content of the proposal. In any case, just remember to stay skin deep, keep them relaxed, and skip right to the things that your proposal accomplishes, which are all positive things for the company, and thus the boss, because approaching this situation in this manner allows you to persuade the boss to accept the proposal while also making sure that the boss does not have to exert a lot of cognitive energy evaluating it, which may cause them to focus on the animals, thus activating their recently deceased pet node.

SIDENOTE

If I were to do something like this, which I actually did during my research by the way, I would show animals, but only as a small part of a larger portrait. I.e., what I personally did was show large game reserves, luscious rainforests, and happy families with pets only being a small part of the overall scene, even though a conservatory style project was the animal-centric meat and potatoes of my entire proposal. I then used inspirational music and quick transitions between the nature/family scenes and images of projections and data to keep my boss's attention where I wanted it and their emotions overall positive. Ergo, they didn't have to pay too much attention to what I was actually saying and just quickly decided that I was "good to go." All because I used the right shallow cues to persuade them.

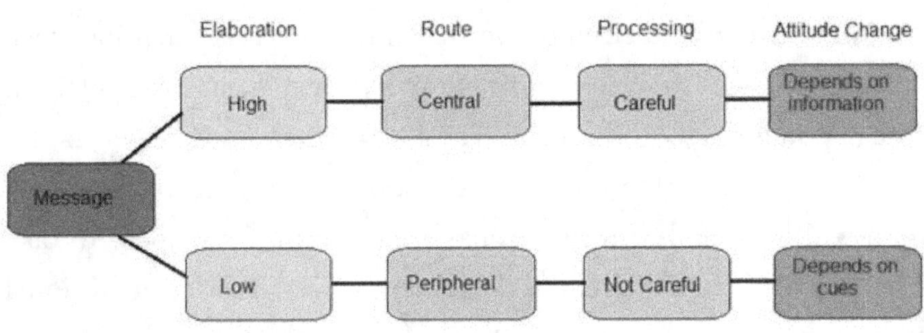

So that was just a quick and simple, down and dirty breakdown of the elaboration likelihood model, but if you want to look deeper into it, again, there are a plethora of references at the end of this book. But at any rate, just so that we are all on the same page, before going on to the other two models I just need you to remember a couple of specific things. Number one, according to the elaboration likelihood model there are two routes when it comes to persuading someone, with the end goal of each being to change their attitude and/or behavior. The first of these is the central route and it involves you drawing the person into the substance of your persuasive position so that they are expending a lot of cognitive resources and/or thinking power evaluating the merits of your position. The second, on the other hand, is the peripheral route of persuasion. This route is when you keep the Subject's cognition at the outer edges of your position. Put another way, you do not, with this route, want their cognition to work very hard. Instead, you want to try and take advantage of heuristics and things that they are familiar with and/or have positive preexisting evaluations of (powerful imagery, music, slogans, etc.) to speed up their encoding and evaluation stages, thus leading to a, yes, more shallow evaluation, but an often equally effective one. In sum, you want them to be "shallow" whilst evaluating your argument.

Number two, and I cannot overstate this, pay special attention when it comes to establishing a baseline of the Subject of your manipulation. The reason is that both the central and peripheral routes of persuasion can be very effective; however, if you establish an incorrect baseline then both will likely fail. This is because which route you choose to take relies heavily on the content of the communication and the emotional state of the Subject (how much they care), and also the external factors surrounding the Subject (how much ability they have to actually think deeply about the object). So, yes, if you have an accurate and thorough baseline evaluation at the ready, then you can pick the appropriate route, strategy, and timing needed to achieve success; but if you do not establish a thorough baseline beforehand, well, good luck to you.

Alright, so moving on, in the academic community the elaboration likelihood model is what is known as a conceptual model. Now I know that this sounds complex, but in reality, it just means that ELM involves an overarching continuum (how much elaboration and likelihood a person is going to have) regarding the individual being manipulated that can be applied to any nonspecific situation. In other words, it is somewhat plug and play. These next two models, on the other hand, are not conceptual models. Rather, they are what the academic community calls structural models, and this basically just means that instead of making one big system that covers every part of the persuasion process in two major aspects (elaboration/ likelihood), they instead break down each individual persuasion into several structural elements.

To begin, the first of these structural models is called the **Yale Attitude Change Approach**. Now this approach/model is, in some ways, primitive in the sense that it has since been updated by the **SMCR model**, but I still want to look at it because it was actually the first structural model of persuasion, and is thus a very important part of that newer models foundation. Anyway, this model, developed by a cohort of psychologists from Yale in the mid-20th century, looked at persuasion as having three main elements. These were *who, what, and whom.* Let me explain.

In 1951 researchers by the names of Dr. Hovland and Dr. Weiss sought to investigate how persuasion occurs among different individuals. To test their hypotheses these two researchers decided to expose experiment participants to several different newspaper articles and magazine clippings that covered a variety of political information, which sounds simple enough, but these researchers also had a trick up their sleeve. This is to say that by the time the participants were exposed to the printed content it had been tampered with. The result, one group saw an article and was then led to believe that it was written by a highly reputable American source while the other group, however, saw the exact same article, but was instead told that it was written by Russian sources.

Well, as you may have guessed, the articles that were perceived to have been written by reputable sources were much more likely to be believed by the participants than the ones that had been "written" by the Soviet sources, even though they were the same stories! Now this finding, for its time, was revolutionary in the field of psychology because is demonstrated quantitatively for the first time ever that *who* is trying to persuade us has a significant amount to do with how successful that persuasion will be, and that perhaps this factor can be more impactful than the information itself. Pretty neat, right?

Anyway, after conducting years of follow-up research, as well as reviewing supplementary works from many more individuals within the cadre of Yale psychologists studying this topic, the Yale Attitude

Change Approach was born. In essence, it showed that the person *who* is doing the persuasion is important, *what* they say is important, and also that *whom* is being persuaded matters; not simply what is being said/read/watched. Case in point, this is where the *who, what, whom* comes from. You see, these Yale psychologists were some of the first to realize that not all dupe's are made equal. I.e., if the messenger is reputable and trustworthy, the message is attractive and logical, but the person receiving the message is not listening because they dislike that messenger, then this persuasion will likely be far less successful than a persuasion wherein the person receiving it is far more interested, even if the duper is not as reputable or the message is not as solid. Ergo, all three of these factors need to be in alignment if your manipulation is to be successful.

SIDENOTE

The reason the Yale Attitude Change Approach is useful is because unlike the ELM, which only has two broad methods for persuading someone (Central/Peripheral routes), the Yale way of doing things breaks everything down into three detailed steps (Though both models can, and in my opinion, should be used together.). In other words, if you use this model, you simply need to evaluate who is saying what to whom, in that order. To illustrate, if I know that the person I am talking to hates me, but also loves the Wall Street Journal, maybe I can still persuade them by using the WSJ as a source, and not myself. For instance, instead of *me* telling them that open borders are bad for the economy, perhaps I will instead tell them about an article in the WSJ that says this. Good to go?

Now at the risk of beating a dead horse, for you lot reading this book this model should also highlight the importance of proper preparation when you approach the planning phase of your manipulation, which if it isn't already obvious will change for each Subject. This is to say that the same approach that worked for one person may not work for another simply because the new person being manipulated is not focusing on the elaboration route, cues, and/or heuristics that you want them to. And this is also another reason why so many of those "How To" books and online programs are bullshit. In other words, the "How To," as these models show, changes with each and every manipulation depending on who is communicating what to whom. I digress though.

Ok, moving on, as I stated previously the Yale Attitude Change a\Approach is slightly outdated, but only because it has since turned into a beautiful persuasive butterfly known as the **SMCR** model of persuasion. Now this newer model has been studied and improved upon by many individuals over the years (again, if you are interested in these folks go to the reference section at the end of this book), but all of these improvers still agree on its basic tenants/elements. Those basic elements are what I want to discuss next.

SIDENOTE

Much like how the Yale Attitude Chance Approach breaks persuasion down into steps, so too does the SMCR model. In other words, you apply each in the same step by step manner when preparing your manipulation strategy, and both can be used in conjunction with the ELM.

To begin, the first of these SMCR elements is **Sender**, and you can think of this element as the replacement for the *who* element of the Yale approach, even though they are both essentially the same. Now when it comes to the details of this element, at the end of the day a good sender must be both trustworthy and credible. Therefore, individuals with more reputable titles and/or names, which allow us to use heuristics to evaluate them positively with very little effort, will have a natural leg up when it comes to persuasion. But in addition to this, it also helps to be likable. This is to say that a lot of new research has shed light on the fact that more attractive, and therefore more likable senders have a natural leg up when it comes to persuasion just as if they possessed documented credibility and trustworthiness. And the reason this is the case is because of something called our biological immune system, which is a part of our evolutionary biology that helps us avoid harmful things and is something that you should either take advantage of or watch out for, depending, put bluntly, on where you think you fall on a scale of one to ten. I.e., if you are ugly (like me), you may need to develop a healthy sense of humor if you want to be seen as trustworthy because this, and not your face will be the thing that makes you overall more likeable. Make sense?

Now in all seriousness, there are actually a lot of things that can make a sender credible, likeable, and/or trustworthy; and once you have a baseline of the social environment you are operating in, you should be able to figure out what these are. This is to say that, although things like official titles and past accomplishments are generally always on the list, if you are in a blue collar environment, perhaps highlighting that you have grit and work ethic will be the way to make you seem more likeable. Or, alternatively, maybe you are a freshman in college and focusing on your academic accomplishments is the way to go. Either way, just remember that when it comes to this element of the SMCR model a persuasive sender needs to be trusted or liked by the person(s) they are manipulating.

Alright, continuing ever onward, the second element of the SMCR is **Message**, and put simply this element is the actual meat and potatoes of your persuasive argument. Now when it comes to this element it is important to remember that the message has to not only be appropriate for the person receiving it, but it also must hold water when and if it is subjected to scrutiny; and this is where some of the cognitive factors that we discussed in the last chapter come in handy. You see, you can pretty much make a logical and reasonable argument for anything. With that said, though, if you have a solid baseline of your Subject then you will know how best to frame and structure the message of your persuasion so that their cognition evaluates it in a way you see fit. To elaborate, if you know that your Subject will be using the central route to evaluate your case then it is best to use an argument you know is logically equal to or superior to the one they will bring forth. In other words, facts over emotions.

Of course, if this is not feasible, then perhaps you will need to try and persuade your Subject using the peripheral route. This would entail structuring and framing your message so that the more illogical portions of your case are less accessible, or visible than the stronger, more emotional aspects of your message. For instance, if you are trying to convince your wife that you need to work, but you actually just want to go out with your buddies, your message should focus on anything else besides how late you will be home. I.e., in this scenario I would trigger their hot cognition, and some nodes about financial gain and stress, by using a highly emotional peripheral persuasion. Case in point, in lieu of talking about the quantitative benefits of me staying out late, I would instead display a high level of excitement about what is going on at work coupled with a mention of how stressed I have been about money. The reason, this strategy of message structuring would draw attention away from how late I will be home to, instead, how I am fixing a stressful situation that affects us both by making beneficial career moves (stress is the focus not financial gain).

Now there are many other ways you could go about handling this same scenario, and many of them would change based on your specific situation, as well as who is involved, but my point is this. When using the peripheral route, tailor your message in a way that will draw the attention of the receiver to only the emotional aspects you want them to see and avoid giving them something to counterargue that they can beat with logic. Afterall, what wife would be so cruel as to kneecap my excitement over work, while also ending my attempts to mitigate my stress? Good to go?

Ok, the third element of the SMCR is **Channel**. Now this one can be a bit ambiguous so make sure you really understand it before moving on. Essentially, this element refers to how an individual receives a message. Of course, this is different from the source element (sender) in that the channel factors vary depending on each individual manipulation. Put another way, this could mean that the same person is giving different people the same message in different ways, and some of these ways, or channel factors if you prefer, are whether the message is delivered in a personal or non-personal way, think about a written memo vs an in-person presentation, whether it is externally paced or internally paced, again, an individual can read a memo at their own pace or hang on for the ride of your presentation, and what the context/environment of the channel is.

When it comes to channel factors, those first two seem pretty self-explanatory, right? Well, for that last one I want you to think about hearing political news from a close friend vs an official media source. Which would be more likely to persuade you? Which would be more likely to persuade your sibling or best friend? You see, the channel factor, or the mode in which information is being relayed, is often overlooked. But is perhaps one of the most important elements of persuasion, and thus why it was included in the SMCR model and subsequently part of the reason why the SMCR model is an improvement over the Yale Attitude Change Approach. Ergo, for the manipulators out their reading and/or listening to this, pay especially close attention to what channel factors your Subject responds to best.

To illustrate what a channel factor is with a personal example, when I was a very young man, I began training in the Jui Jitsu and Muay Thai martial arts; and I even continued this training into adulthood, the military, and occasionally dust off the ole gloves and mitts from time to time to this day. Needless to say, I know a fair amount about fighting and have for a long time. Despite this depth of knowledge, though, a male role model I have had in my life for a long time, whom I enjoyed watching UFC events with as a young man, would never listen to a word I had to say in regard to what the fighters on the TV were doing wrong. This is to say that it would become endlessly frustrating to me that they would not listen to me even as I said the same things the announcers were saying, and I wanted to remedy this problem. So, I decided to try something new (I guess this is a point for the nature side of the nature vs nurture argument because even as a young man I was inquisitive about human behavior.).

To solve this annoying problem what I started doing was adjusting the framing of my commentary about the fights so that it appeared I had gotten my information from the commentators earlier in the night. For instance, if I noticed one fighter was not defending his lead leg, I would say that the announcer brought up the fighter's lack of leg kick defense and it is something we should pay attention to, thus making the information come from a different channel than simply my own thoughts. Well, sure enough, shortly thereafter when the fighter would start to have their leg ravaged by kicks, the individual I was watching the fights with would look at me and say, "You called it."

Anyway, not long after that moment the individual I always watched the fights with started to inquire about my thoughts on the fighters on a regular basis; and I bring this up because it not only shows how the channel factor, in my case making the information come from a reputable source and not me, is important, but also because it shows how channel factors can change the individuals' evaluations of you as the manipulator moving forward. In other words, after changing the channel for my fight commentary I had, essentially, changed their evaluation of me so that they could now use heuristics to determine that what I was saying was accurate; and the result of this was that if I needed to do any manipulating/persuading related to fight commentary, let's say move the individual to make certain bets with confidence, I could have started to do this using the peripheral route of persuasion instead of the central route, which, as previously discussed is often the most effective route because it means that the Subject is less focused on what you are doing and/or saying, and more focused on shallow cues like heuristics.

Ok, moving on, the final SMCR factor is **Receiver**, and this element is, essentially, the same thing as the *whom* element of the

Yale model. Furthermore, it, like all the others, is one that cannot be overlooked. Now to begin our discussion of this element, as we talked about in the Yale Attitude Change Approach section, the *whom* (receiver) can have many factors that make them unique in regard to each individual manipulation; and this makes the receiver the element of the SMCR that the baseline concept has the most effect upon. In other words, you need to know the baseline of your receiver before you can even begin to formulate a solid strategy for using the other factors of persuasion or elements of the manipulation process as a whole. Case in point, are there certain issues that they feel strongly about and will use heuristics or motivated reasoning with? Are they highly distracted right now or in the extremely high/low IQ range? Are they likely to use hot cognition or are they a more methodological thinker?

You see, all of these things must be accounted for before you can choose whether to use the central or peripheral route, how to structure your message, and what channel to use to communicate that message. But in addition to all of these, and this is where the receiver element can become extremely tricky, you have to make sure that your message and channel are structured specifically to the individual you are persuading so that you keep them out of their surveillance system. I.e., in the UFC scenario, if I was to reference a commentator that the individual hated, then it is highly unlikely that they would accept the information because that individual would see the information I presented as threatening. All because it came from a source that is, in their perceived reality, either unlikable, untrustworthy, and/or not credible. Thus why you must take into account who the receiver of your persuasion is when preparing your strategy. Capeesh?

Alright, I know that was a lot I just threw at you, but believe me, it was necessary and worth it. That said, since we have covered the three academic models of persuasion, I want to move on and discuss two topics that will help you practically use these models in real life. Sound like a plan? Sweet.

<table>
<tr><td>Sender</td><td>Message</td><td>Channel</td><td>Receiver</td></tr>
</table>

So without further to do, the first topic I want to discuss in this next section is **social judgement theory**, which was developed by Dr. Muzafer Sherif in 1961. In lay terms, this theory attempts to conceptualize how our attitudes move and how resilient they are to change. Now for this theory I want you to imagine a thick line on a piece of paper. Essentially, this line represents the entire continuum of attitudes, both the positive end and the negative end, surrounding an individual issue (see the next illustration). For simplicity, in this illustration we will use your attitude about a movie.

Next, imagine that on one end of the line you have pure hatred of the movie and on the other you have complete adoration of the movie. Now, imagine that this line is divided into three sections with, typically, the middle one being the smallest and the outermost being the biggest, and that the middle most, wherever that is, is green and has a big anchor in the middle of it. This green zone is called your latitude of acceptance and the anchor is where your current attitude is. For the sake of argument, let's say that the anchor is slightly to the left, or hatred side of the center.

SIDENOTE

It may be very easy for your attitude to move around slightly within the latitude of acceptance because these are attitude positions very similar to the one you already have. For instance, let's say that your anchor is slightly closer to the left side of the line, which is the side for hatred. This means that you do not like the movie, and with persuasion you could easily move to like it or dislike it a little bit more because this would not completely uproot your prior held attitude (Remember that attitudes are just the most up to date cognitive evaluations you have made regarding an object.).

Now let's say that you look outside of this green zone. What you will see is that there is a second section that is larger than the middle one and also yellow. This section is called your latitude of noncommitment, and this zone represents attitudes that are outside of your comfort zone, but also not necessarily threatening. Now when it comes to this particular movie, wherein your current attitude, as we said above, is slightly to the hatred side, this zone would represent the attitudes of indifference and moderate dislike of the movie. In other words, the right side of your latitude of noncommitment would be in the middle (indifference) and the left side would be in the middle of the left side (moderate dislike).

Outside of this zone is your latitude of rejection and it is red. Also, technically speaking, this is the overall biggest zone even though it may actually be very small on one side, depending, of course, on where your current attitude is to begin with (again, see next illustration). Now, for this example, the movie example that is, the leftmost side of the line would be red. This represents pure hatred of the movie and if someone tried to convince you of this, their argument would likely not sway you because attitudes in this zone are so far away from your current attitude that they are very threatening. In other words, if someone did try to persuade you to hate the movie, you would probably stay in the, "I didn't really like it, but it wasn't that bad" zone instead of going all the way to the hatred zone, because it's just too unfamiliar.

Now on the right side of this movie line, a large portion would also be red as well. Much more, in fact, than is red on the left side of the line, and this is because your initial attitude is slightly to the left. Ergo, the latitude of noncommitment gets you across the halfway point, but most of the positive positions will still be quite far from your initial attitude, and therefore, threatening. Furthermore, anyone trying to move your attitude so that it is positive toward the movie would likely fail because, just like if they tried to move you to the pure hatred side, this side is just too far from your original attitude position and/or latitude of acceptance. Make sense?

Social Judgement Theory

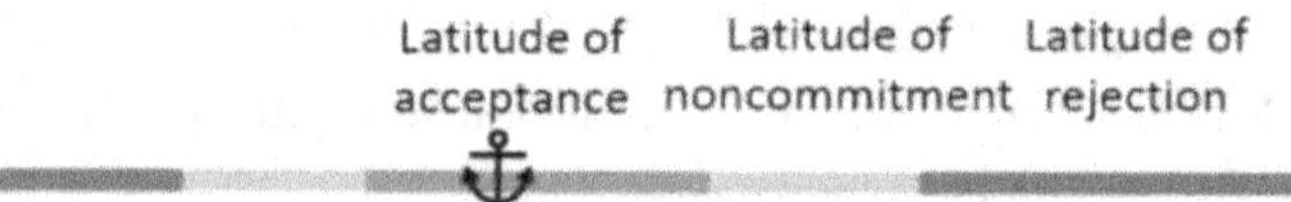

Now while on this topic, it is worth mentioning that the size of each section can actually change significantly depending on how strongly you feel about an issue. I.e., in the example of the movie, for instance, it is likely that you will not have a heavy emotional investment when it comes to making an evaluation of the film because it isn't that big of a deal, and because of this your latitude of acceptance could be rather large. In fact, when it comes to something you don't care about all that much, your latitude of acceptance and your latitude of noncommitment may even be far larger than your latitude of rejection, and this would mean that you could be persuaded to change your attitude about this object rather easily if someone attempted to manipulate you. Of course, the inverse is true as well. Case in point, if, for instance, instead of a movie we were discussing abortion, the amount you care about the issue, which is referred to as ego involvement, would likely be much higher, thus resulting in a much smaller latitude of acceptance, a much smaller latitude of noncommitment, and a much larger latitude of rejection. Good to go?

Social Judgement Theory Cont.

Low ego involvement

High ego involvement

So the reason I bring this theory up is because you can use it to illustrate in your mind how the persuasion process should actually work. To elaborate, research has shown that persuasion is best accomplished through locating an individual's latitude of noncommitment on as issue and then trying to move them there, through whatever manipulation strategy you have deemed correct for that individual person and issue, over an extended period of time. You see, if you stay within the individual's latitude of acceptance, they do not really register the new attitude as different from their own preexisting attitude, and therefore, may just choose to stay where they are. However, if you try to move them to their latitude of rejection, well, good fuckin luck buddy.

Alright, to sum this topic up, as a manipulator your goal, when persuading someone of something that is, should be to establish a baseline assessment of their social judgement theory line in regard to the topic at hand, and then a subsequent manipulation strategy (one that factors in the individual elements involved and the preferred route) that aims to move that individual to their latitude of noncommitment. The reason, this will make their baseline change just enough so that they are now secure in this new position, which is noticeably different from their previous one, but not so far away that it is threatening. And just food for thought, if you continue to work on them in this way, eventually you will be able to incrementally move them to where you want without them feeling pressured. Of course, as you may have guessed this can take some time, but then again, I never promised you a quick and easy path to success, only an effective one.

Ok, moving on, the second topic that will help you understand how to use the models of persuasion will not be quite as longwinded as the first; but nonetheless it is, in my opinion, a vital piece of the puzzle. At any rate, this next topic is called **argument order**.

To begin, you need to understand that this topic refers specifically to the message aspect of the persuasion models. I say this because argument order, in essence, refers to when the receiver actually receives the meat and potatoes (friction point) of your persuasion. Now this does not mean what time of the day mind you, well, not technically, but rather when you let the cat out of the proverbial bag during your overall manipulation. Don't worry, I know this is confusing, but give it a minute and try to hang on until you get to the illustration.

Put plainly, there are two main aspects to consider for a discussion on this topic; and the first of these is the timing structure of your individual persuasion, which is referred to as the **within-message order**, and the second is the structure of your overall manipulation in relation to the persuasive manipulations of others, which is called the **between-messages order**. To simplify, within-message order means how you structure the actual message itself, and between-message order means when you choose to use this message. Make sense? I didn't think so. Let me break these down separately to make them a little less confusing.

So, when I talk about the structure of your individual persuasion (within-message order) what I mean is, put simply, where does the friction point exist. This is to say that at some point in every manipulation you actually have to make something happen. In other words, if you want to convince someone of something, then there will be a time when the other foot drops and you actually try to compel them. To illustrate this with a more sinister example than my previous ones, imagine that you have been cheating on your significant other and one of your mutual friends from another couple recently saw you in public with the person you were cheating with. Because this witness is so close to you and your significant other, you know that confrontation with your partner is inevitable and that at some point you will need to plead your case in order to manipulate them into believing that you were not, in fact, cheating.

Regardless of whatever story you have cooked up to defend yourself, when it comes to the within-message order there are three ways to organize it. The first of these ways is what is known as the **climax** within-message order. In essence this structure involves starting slow and building up to the friction point. I.e., when the confrontation does happen, if your plan is to tell your significant other that the person you were with is a work colleague, then this type of within-message organization would entail you drawing them in by talking about how much you have been working, how you have had to be out of the house a lot and that this should be no surprise, and then ending with the friction point (persuasive case). In this situation, the friction point is addressing the uncomfortable issue at hand and telling your significant other that the individual is just a coworker and that they simply have the wrong idea. In sum, you start slow and end with a bang, well, I guess in this scenario you actually started with the bang…. boom…nailed it. Oh, but then again you nailed it too. Ok, I'll stop.

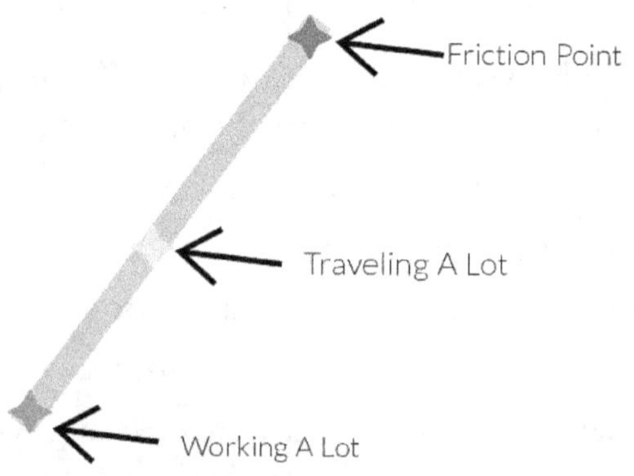

CLIMAX WITHIN-MESSAGE ORDER

Continuing on, the second structure that you could use for organizing your persuasive message is called the **anti-climax** within-message order. Put bluntly, this organization style is, as it sounds, the complete opposite of the climax structure. To elaborate using this same infidelity scenario, a message that resembles an anti-climax argument would consist of you coming right out of the gate hard and telling your significant other that the individual you were seen with was a work colleague and that nothing sinister was at play. You would then follow this up by explaining that work was busy, you did not think they found it interesting, and therefore didn't think the work relationship/get-togethers were worthy of disclosing. In other words, starting with a bang and then moving into the less serious/uncomfortable information.

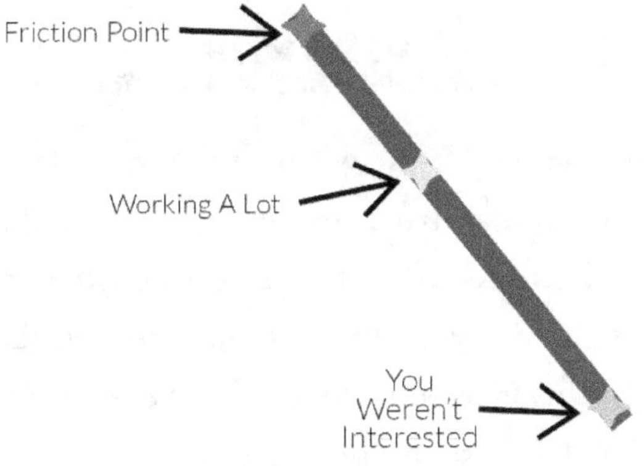

**ANTI-CLIMAX
WITHIN-MESSAGE ORDER**

The third way of structurally organizing your message is by using what is called the **pyramidal** within-message order. Put plainly, this style of organization involves starting slow, building up to the friction point, and then tapering off. For example, when it comes to this cheating scenario you would first talk about how work has been busy, then you would drop the fact that the individual you were seen with is just a coworker (friction point), and then, finally, you would end off softly by explaining that you did not think that your significant other was even interested in your work situation. In other words, in this within-message order structure you start off slow and easy, then make a bang, and then after that you go back to the comfortable stuff.

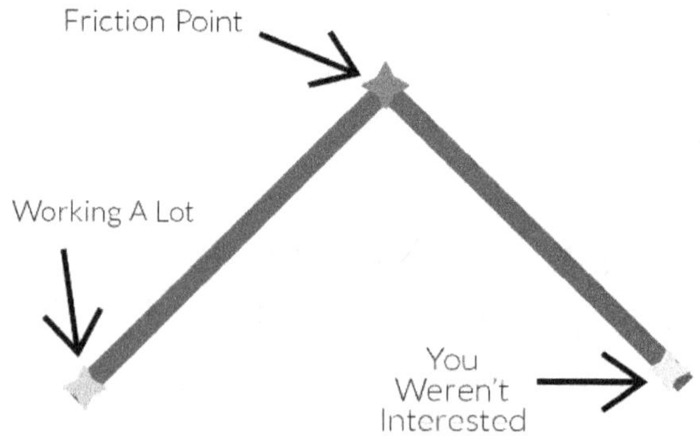

PYRAMIDAL
WITHIN-MESSAGE ORDER

Now when it comes to the within-message order, even though it seems like the pyramidal structure would be the best, mainly because it sandwiches the friction point in between two softer layers of communication, in reality the data actually supports the opposite idea. In other words, this is technically the least effective within-message order, and what has actually been shown to be true is that either a climax or anti-climax within-message structure is most effective when manipulating and/or persuading. Of course, all of the other factors, such as the channel, context, what route you are using, and what route the Subject's cognition is using all come into play as well; but with that said the fact remains that if you can either frontload or backload the friction point of your manipulation you will likely have more success. Pretty wild, right?

Ok, before we close out this section and move on to the final one, in regard to that aforementioned scenario, my advice to you when it comes to the within-message order would be to first establish what type of cognition the significant other is likely to use. I.e., do they fly off the handle and scream when they are angry or do they shut down and get quiet. You see, how they behave will determine when you should lay out your persuasive argument. In lay terms, choose the order that, in your situation, gives the message the highest chance of being processed by the other person's cognition (when they are most reasonable).

SIDENOTE

In a broader context, imagine that you are speaking to a boardroom? Well, figure out if they take a minute to put down their phones and pay attention (a situation where you would choose a climax within-message order), or if they ready to go right away and will lose interest quickly if you do not grab their attention (a situation that would require an anti-climax within-message order).

Alright, we are almost done folks, so bear with me. The second part of the order of arguments concept is between-message order, and it has two internal elements. Now, for a little context, this aspect of persuasion comes into play when there are multiple competing persuasions going on. What I mean by this is that between-message order refers to where your persuasion is in relation to the competition's arguments. Simple enough, yeah?

An easy way to think about this concept is in terms of politics. For example, when deciding when to schedule a campaign rally a candidate should take into consideration when the other candidates are speaking at that same location during the available window. The reason is that if the opposing candidate is speaking in the same location around the same time as you, you would want to schedule your rally a day or two before theirs. This is because of the **primacy effect**, which is the first internal element of between-message order.

In essence, the primacy effect states that when two competing persuasions are operating close to one another, the one experienced first will have a stronger impact on the person or group of persons being manipulated (in the cheating scenario this would mean that you should boot, scoot, and boogie to reach your significant other before their friend does). Taking this into consideration, it would behoove the candidate planning a rally to speak to the voting bloc before their competitor because this will mean that their message will have a more potent and long lasting effect. In this way, you can think of it as tainting the persuasive waters with your lingering message.

The second internal element of the between-message order concept, on the other hand, is the **recency effect**. To illustrate this element, if the opposing candidate *was* speaking during the same time frame that you want to speak, and you could not get scheduled before them, then you would want to hold off and come back to that area a few months down the line; and this is because the recency effect posits that when there is a great deal of distance in between two competing persuasions, the latter is going to be more effective. Ergo, if you did not wait it would be as if you, not your competitor was the one swimming in tainted waters. Furthermore, because you did not wait you were unable to undo the tainting, thus making your message less effective. Of course, if you were, however, to take my advice and wait to return to the area a few months later, well, then your message would actually have a far greater and more lasting impact on the voting bloc than that of your competitors because, according to the recency effect, enough time would have passed between messages that you would be able to, essentially, "untaint" the persuasive waters in your favor.

Now in a non-political situation, let's use the board room presentation example again, trying to use the recency effect and presenting your proposal after your competition's proposals would actually be a very bad idea. Rather, you would be better off taking the short term loss and rescheduling your presentation because, assuming that all of the manipulation factors (and baselines) were properly accounted for, and your within-message order was solid, this would give you a far greater chance of achieving success. Of course, this is not always possible, so, if rescheduling is simply not feasible then you will need to instead use all of the models and factors discussed in the last two chapters to persuade your competitors to go after you during the boardroom presentations so that you can use the primacy effect. If you wanted the best between-message order for your persuasion that is.

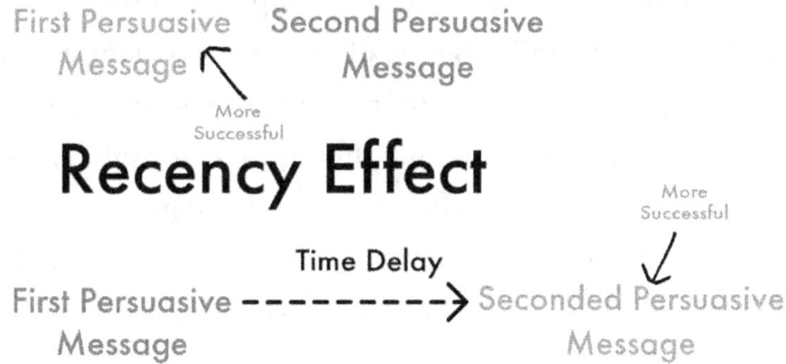

Ok, by this point you should have a pretty good grasp on how attitudes and behaviors work together, the three academic models of persuasion, what social judgement theory is and how to apply it, as well as some factors related to the order of arguments. When used in conjunction these principles and concepts will be extremely beneficial to you as you change from a dupe caterpillar into a beautiful and majestic manipulative butterfly. So, take them to heart.

Now, as a final addendum I would be remiss if I did not point you in the direction of Dr. Robert Cialdini. Put plainly, Dr. Cialdini is a published Ph.D. who hails from my alma mater of Arizona State University, and he wrote a book in 2008 called *Influence: Science and Practice.* Now this book is far too in depth to cover here, and thus why I chose not to include it, but I would highly advise reading it if you have enjoyed this book so far and want a book that is more specific about the "How To" techniques of manipulation (I.e., the foot in the door technique and the mere exposure effect). This is because the six principles of persuasion covered in his work apply to both changing an individual's behavior through persuasion of their attitude, as well as persuading someone's attitude through creating a change in their behavior, which, I'll admit is a bit sexier than what I am doing here. I mean, as I have stated before, my book exists simply to provide you with a framework for manipulation by explaining it in a broader context, while also detailing certain structural elements of the process, like the academic models of persuasion and my 4 dimensions of lying. With that said, though, a highly influential piece of my research was Dr. Cialdini's book and it contains six specific strategies for persuading people. Ergo, taking what you learn in this book and applying those strategies to it would greatly enhance your manipulative ability and is a far better plan than paying $49.99 a month for some online forum that purports to teach you the keys to achieving manipulative success (looking at you Hustler University). So, yeah, check it out.

Well, now that I have given a free plug away (Full disclosure I have never even spoken to Dr. Cialdini), I think it is time to go. In closing, first figure out whether you need to alter someone's attitude or their behavior, then utilize the elements and routes contained in the academic models of persuasion to structure a strong manipulation strategy, and finally, use all of this and the proper order of argument combination to move them, through communication, into whatever issue-specific latitude of noncommitment that you need to find success in your final manipulative goal.

Ok, that's it folks. See you in the next chapter wherein we will be discussing my novel research regarding the six archetypes of power.

What is Power

"Elevation, it seems, is in some way a mile marker of human accomplishment. Not only in status, but also actual and literal elevation. Instagram selfies on planes, planting a flag on the moon, Everest expeditions, and yoga poses on the edge of great drops. Humans certainly are fascinated with heights, aren't we? Fuck, Heaven itself, a place categorized as a place far above us in the sky, is seen as the ultimate paradise. All the while the fear of a buried Hell lingers within and burns the neural pathways deep within our subconscious. Does this represent something more; is elevating oneself in one way or another the ultimate goal for those with and without ambition alike? **—Alexander Oakes**

What we have covered so far in this book, aside from our earlier sidebars into the worlds of philosophy and ethics that is, has been based on qualitative and quantitative research done by either me or already established scholars. What are these two types of research though? Well, if you go and do a quick Google search Wikipedia will tell you that quantitative research is *a research strategy that focuses on quantifying the collection and analysis of data.*

It is formed from a deductive approach where emphasis is placed on the testing of theory, shaped by empiricist and positivist philosophies. Now, I know that sounds complicated, but this is basically just a fancy way of saying that it is a method of research that crunches numbers and uses hard data to prove hypotheses; and this is similar in some ways, but overall very different from qualitative research. Case in point, if you type qualitative research into that same search bar you used before, once again Google will direct you to Wikipedia, wherein qualitative research is defined as *a type of research that aims to gather and analyze non-numerical (descriptive) data in order to gain an understanding of individuals' social reality, including understanding their attitudes, beliefs, and motivation. This type of research typically involves in-depth interviews, focus groups, or observations in order to collect data that is rich in detail and context. Qualitative research is often used to explore complex phenomena or to gain insight into people's experiences and perspectives on a particular topic. It is particularly useful when researchers want to understand the meaning that people attach to their experiences or when they want to uncover the underlying reasons for people's behavior.* In other words, collecting qualitative data, unlike quantitative research, is more about taking a long chunk of time and submerging yourself into the object and/or environment that you want to research.

Now, the reason I bring all of this up here at the beginning of the chapter is because this chapter, as well as the next one, covers the new research I bring to the table when it comes to communication, manipulation, and persuasion. This is to say that even though this entire book as a whole provides a somewhat new and unique perspective on these topics, which also required a significant amount of research across various fields I might add, this chapter in particular was the product of a multi-year qualitative study I conducted wherein

I decided to first see what causes people to attain power, and then how they change when they receive that power. To that end, even though the findings that are presented in this chapter did not come from measurable quantitative research, as the next chapter did and also all of the chapters up until this point, they should still not be discounted and skipped over as pseudo-science. The reason, qualitative studies are a very important part of social sciences research and with them, as I have done here, we can gain a lot of insight into things that are difficult and/or even impossible to measure, like personality archetypes, for instance.

Alright, with that preamble out of the way, let's get into this thing. We will start by talking about what I believe is an important part of the human puzzle that helps explain why some people who should have power don't, and why some people who should not have power do. Good to go? Great.

To begin, are all people created equal? I mean, we certainly like to think so, but what does equal actually mean? Well, if we are talking about the value of each person through the lens of generally accepted Western moral standards, then yes, each life is precious, and none is more valuable than the other. Hell, as the frontier of human rights and individual liberty, the United States even has this belief woven into the very fabric of our founding documents.

"We hold these truths to be self-evident, that all men are created equal, that they are endowed by their Creator with certain unalienable Rights, that among these are Life, Liberty and the pursuit of Happiness".

Seems fair enough to me, however, true equity has never, including in the West, been achieved among humans in terms of wealth, power, and/or quality of life. So, if we are truly equal then why the hell are so many people broke, and will we ever find true equality as a species and culture (This paragraph makes me seem like some sort of communist. Definitely not!)? Unfortunately, I find it very unlikely, and in fact, I believe that inequality will continue to increase as human societies advance. To that end, if I am right and this grim prediction *is* true, then it would greatly benefit you to examine how you fit into an ever-changing social structure so that you can increase your societal value and accomplish your overall goals. Furthermore, and more importantly for this book mind you, if I am right then you should seek to better understand how the power structures of our social environment operate on the level of the individual so that you can learn how to use them to your advantage.

Anyway, moving on, all life is valuable and no life has inherently more worth than any other. This is what we just agreed upon, yes? Well, you and I are not alone. This is to say that in our modern environment this sentiment is now agreed upon by the vast majority of people living in the Western world. Be that as it may, though, the harsh reality is that in the real world, and not the ideological utopia we all pretend we live in, people's worth to a society more realistically exists as a product of and changes based upon what they actually provide for that society; and it is worthy of note that this relationship exists despite what those people could potentially contribute given different circumstances and has been the status quo since as far back as hunter/gatherer societies.

You see, before agriculture, roughly 10,000 years ago, tribes and communities created internal social hierarchies that gave lesser status to individuals that were deemed to be less beneficial to the in-group

(Anyone else thinking about the movie Year One with Jack Black?). Meanwhile, on the other side of the social hierarchy, the members of the in-group that the tribes and communities believed to be the most societally beneficial received a very high level of rewards, resources, and social status for their efforts. I.e., the best hunters received the first pass at communal meals, had their basic needs met with servants or slaves, and attracted the most fertile women, while the least skilled hunters had to settle for scraps at the dinner table, and when it came to women, whatever was around at the pre-agriculture version of last call. Make sense?

Well, in the 10,000 years since then, speaking bluntly, not a goddamn thing has significantly changed. In fact, the only difference now is what societies place value on and how we gain power and/ or social status within those societies. Or put another way, instead of a fresh deer and protection, societies now place value on green paper and how many followers you have. But with this said, even though *how* we distribute/allot value has changed, just know that regardless of what we place value on, as the needs and norms of a society change and progress there will still always be a social hierarchy that is directly related to and structured around the contributions of those within it. Ergo, those that make valuable contributions will receive success and power, thus putting them at the top of that aforementioned social hierarchy, and those who do not make valuable contributions will be at the bottom because a person's position in this social hierarchy, as mentioned above, is a direct causation of what they provide for that society; and just FYI, this dynamic plays out among smaller in-groups and social environments, like friend groups, families, and bands the very same way.

SIDENOTE

I use the terms in-group and out-group several times in this book. These are very simple concepts from social identity theory and evolutionary biology. To explain, in-group basically states that whatever groups we are a part of are our in-groups. I.e., our political party of choice (Libertarian), our family (Oakes), and the country of our citizenship (Merican) are all examples of in-groups and you can be a part of many of them. Out-group, on the other hand, means the inverse of this. I.e., your out-group(s) is/are any group(s) that is/are not part of one of your in-groups (If you are a Republican, the Democrats are your out-group.).

Now before going any further, if right now you are thinking I am insane because there are a lot of useless and untalented people out there killing it, well, as every failed comedian and/or untalented actor has forgotten to recognize during their angry outbursts about "fairness" on social media, you have to understand that the supply and demand of social status, as well as the power that comes with it within a society, is not always founded on "actual" value. Case in point, one of the most successful accounts on YouTube, for instance, is a small child opening presents. "Well, what the hell is he doing for society" you say as you throw your phone across your dingy apartment that you pay for by cleaning out the sewers so that we can all shit in peace and comfort. The answer is simple. Put plainly, he is one of the few influencers who made it in that line of work and is occupying millions of children while their parents take a power nap and advertisers push their products. Make sense?

Examples like this suggest that the demand for contribution, as it turns out, doesn't have to be for necessities like food, water, and/or protection anymore. Therefore, people who actually do very little for the in-group can actually achieve a very high position in society's hierarchy because what that society places value on has changed with advancement. In this way, I suppose you could look at it like the ability to take the important things for granted is one of the blessings and curses of living in the very comfortable 21st century wherein which contributions are most valuable can be surprising, and in some instances, downright depressing…. looking at you, influencers.

Any who, to stay on track, like that little kid making millions on YouTube, what worth we provide to society spans a wide range and changes as society changes. Now, of course, some of the obvious high-worth positions in our current society are one's in the STEM fields, one's in government service (though I would argue that these positions are largely just useless bureaucratic appointments that leech off of the rest of us while providing nothing in return), and ones in the Hollywood entertainment industry; but what about garbage men and police officers? I mean, without their services our society would likely fall apart and descend into a landfill of violence and chaos, would they not? Well, even though it is true that we need these less-glamourous fields far more than, say, the Hollywood elites, the fact that society would be objectively worse off without garbage men and police officers than it would without movie stars is irrelevant due to, essentially, how good we have it. This is to say that because we are not explicitly concerned with survival anymore, societies' hierarchy of status and power has placed these more necessary positions toward the bottom of the proverbial totem pole, and this is all because of societies' supply and demand. In other words, as counterintuitive as it sounds, it is much easier to be in those, very admittedly more admirable and difficult professions, than it is to become an A-list actor or actress because there are simply far more positions and far less competition in these fields. Thus, as a result of the laws of supply and demand, we can therefore expect to have many more people becoming police officers and garbage people than we can people becoming A-list celebrities. Conversely, though, if Hollywood movies all of a sudden started paying minimum wage and governments decided to pay police officers and garbage men seven-figure salaries, we would see this situation reverse itself, and quickly I might add. Put another way, if this happened then a massive influx of high-quality candidates would swarm these fields, thus making them highly competitive and much harder to get into because there would be too much supply for the demand.

Ok, continuing onward, while writing this chapter and thinking about societies' supply and demand I ended up remembering some experiences I had from back when I was in the military. This is to say that when I was stationed in California and went to parties on the coast every weekend, it seemed like every Uber driver I had was some form or another of aspiring performer. One time I asked one of these drivers how long he had been at it. He was an older gentleman of maybe his mid-fifties, so I assumed he had retired and was doing this as a second act while collecting monthly pension paychecks.

But this was not the case and I was shocked when he instead told me that he had been in Los Angeles for 22 years waiting for his big break, and that the thing about acting was, "You either have it or you don't. I got it I just need that big audition." Well, to date he has never landed that audition and I am willing to bet that if he does, he will not "have it," as they say.

Now, the reason I bring all of this up, and the reason it is important to understand my way of looking at people's worth and how that is different from their current social status, is because I do not want you to underestimate or overestimate a person's potential worth (a concept we will cover shortly). You see, if you miscalculate someone's potential worth based on their current actual worth, you may find that your chosen strategy of manipulation was not the correct one. For instance, if you underestimate a barista's potential worth because of their current worth, you may choose to manipulate them using the peripheral route. But what happens when they are actually a Ph.D. student and use, unbeknownst to you, a more central approach in their thinking, which would, as discussed in the last chapter, require you to use the central route of persuasion and not the shallower peripheral route? Or, alternatively, what happens when you try to use the central route on a Ph.D. professor only to find out that they are a moron who is only where they are because they are fishing buddies with the Dean? Anyway, my point is this, if you do not understand how to interpret societies social hierarchy, then you may accidentally make an inaccurate baseline assessment of your Subject, which will ultimately lead to a flawed manipulation strategy. So, look at each person as a clean slate when you meet them.

Ok, I think we have spent enough establishing how people's worth and subsequent status is established within society, as well as why some "worthless" positions still translate into high social status. Moving on from that, for the purposes of my research, and something that is an important addition to this overall worth concept, at least when talking about manipulation that is, I have divided up what worth each person possesses within a society into two categories. The first is **actual worth** and it is exactly what it sounds like. I.e., actual worth can be looked at as a person's worth on paper, their worth to the casual observer, and in practice what they provide to everyone else in the world, as well as their specific societal in-group. Case in point, a theoretical physicist provides groundbreaking ideas, discoveries, and lectures. A successful author provides books people will buy and read, a Congress person provides legislation and votes on national issues, and a pizza delivery driver provides, well, pizza. Ergo, to harken back to societies contribution supply and demand, our actual worth is calculated by combining what we provide to society (which, don't forget, is dependent upon what that society values) and the amount of people who can provide that same contribution at the same level.

Now I recognize that this can be uncomfortable to think about for those of us with low actual worth in our social environment, but nonetheless it is just an inescapable fact of humanity that stems from evolutionary competition, and one that you should accept. For example, I have accepted this bitter pill and have no shame in stating that right now at this very moment Elon Musk is objectively more valuable to society than I am. I mean, sure, stripped bare our lives are perhaps morally equal, but our actual worths, within the confines of this particular society that is, are vastly different; and this has always been the case and will be long after you and me, so I am not butthurt about it…. well, not always anyway.

Alright, moving on, the second category, and the far more important one for budding manipulators of perceived reality like you and the rest of the readers/listeners, is **potential worth**. In lay terms, potential worth is, essentially, the sum of your natural genetic capabilities and the environmental factors around you that influence your life. In other words, your potential worth is what you are biologically capable of accomplishing, given the right environment; and I include both genetics and environment in this definition because endless twin studies have been conducted within the social sciences and all of them show that each of these factors do impact our behavior and the trajectory of our lives, though to differing degrees depending on the person.

To make this a bit clearer, think of it this way. Someone who *could* be a chess grandmaster based on their natural ability may never end up having an opportunity to be around a chess board. Ergo, because their natural ability was not recognized and/or fostered maybe this potential chess wizard becomes an electrician instead, even if they do technically still have all of the natural ability, and IQ to be a world champion. Now contrast that with someone who is not nearly as gifted as that person. Perhaps this person grows up in a family that has the resources to pay for private chess tutors, memberships to formal chess clubs, and whatever else chess nerds do until, through lots of hard work, they eventually reach the level of grandmaster. My point is this. Yes, they have the position and admittedly are very good at chess, but their potential worth, in relation to chess, is actually far lower than the first person's, even though their actual worth in relation to chess is much higher. Make sense?

Granted, this is only an abstract example, so I get that it seems somewhat useless, but what if instead of chess the skill in question was reading people? For instance, a corporate recruiter you need to impress to get a job may be very bad at reading people while their secretary, whom they go to in order to gain deeper insights about candidates, is actually very good at reading people. Did you act differently in the waiting room around the secretary because she wasn't the big boss? Did you say something rude or demeaning to them that would mess up your manipulation with the boss?

These two examples show how our environment can step in and put us in a position that is not necessarily indicative of our actual genetic ability, in regard, that is, to whatever skillset we are talking about. Of course, with that said, which one of these, environment, or genetic ability is more impactful on our development has spurred heated debates in the realm of politics, economics, and social justice, but nonetheless, no one denies that they both play some role in our future. In other words, most people in the social sciences tend to believe that a majority of what you do in life is determined by both nature and nurture, not just one or the other. I digress though.

For the purposes of this book it really doesn't matter which one is more impactful (nature or nurture), all you need to know is that people are not technically equal in worth and that understanding the two types of worth is a crucial aspect of how you approach a Subject you wish to manipulate. I.e., do not assume anyone is where they are simply because of their natural biological ability because gifts like high IQ, natural people-reading skills, and an affinity for deception are things that anyone could have and they can bite you in the ass if you don't see them coming simply because you overlooked a potential threat!

Alright, to keep things rolling along, taking the time to recognize people with high potential worth is an important part of "sizing up" a person you may want to manipulate, as well as anyone in their

Societal Hierarchy

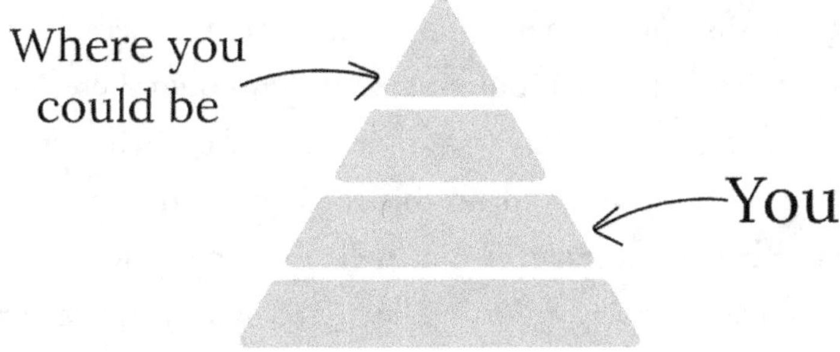

environment that may have an influence over that person; and as I said in chapter one, during my research I had to learn this the hard way by being caught off guard several times by individuals whom I had underestimated. Now I don't want to go down a whole rabbit hole with that again, but my point is that after these humbling experiences I realized that, for example, a janitor could be far more intelligent than a multi-millionaire property developer, and that their actual societal worth was not a good metric for determining a manipulation strategy for them.

To elaborate, maybe the Millionaire was born into a wealthy family that valued education while the janitor was abused their entire life and, as a result, dropped out of school to escape their environment, despite both having the same level of IQ. It would be incorrect, therefore, to assume that I could use the peripheral route on the janitor and the central route on the millionaire because their genetic gifts, at least the ones relevant to manipulation (i.e., reading people, sousing out deception, and attention to detail), may not reflect their actual worth within our society. This is all to say that you just don't know what cognitive processing ability people are capable of based solely on their actual worth. And furthermore, in addition to the risk of a failed manipulation, which is bad enough in its own right, I should also point out that by underestimating the janitor you yourself could also become susceptible to manipulation from them because, after all, all communication is manipulation, and they could therefore decide to communicate with you as a means to the end of their own personal goals the same as you could do this to them; and this is especially true given that a manipulator is at their most dangerous when they are not seen as a threat and/or intellectual equal by the person being manipulated. At any rate, you get the point, but to quickly summarize, to avoid running into this type of problem you want to do your best to avoid showing all of your potential worth to the Subject of your manipulation while also making sure not to overlook theirs, or anyone else's for that matter. Case in point, as Sun Tzu said, "Appear weak when you are strong and strong when you are weak."

Ok, moving on there is, however, another side of the coin when it comes to miscalculating someone's potential worth. This is to say that while trying to alter their perceived reality, just like underestimating someone can lead to an improperly structured strategy, so too can overestimating someone. Take, for instance, someone in a position of authority. Maybe it is a big time corporate executive who oversees your daily duties or even a general manager at a small local restaurant you are working at. Whatever the case, it is often our belief that these people, those who are in positions of power, got there because they are, at least in some way, above average when it comes to either IQ or ability. Well, and this is something that all of my veteran readers and/or listeners know all too well, the reality is that many times people in positions of authority are only there because, to put it bluntly, they simply stuck around longer than anyone else cared to.

You see, merit is generally not the sole determining factor when it comes to achieving status. This is to say that when leaders are being chosen personal relationships, inter-group politics, and candidate availability (supply and demand) all creep into the mix and, in many cases, weigh the scales one way or the other. And this formation of your social groups' power structure is not limited to boardrooms either. For clarity, all of these factors can determine who is the dominant person in your personal relationships, who are the dominant members of your church, who are the dominant members in your group of friends, etc. I digress though.

The key takeaway is that you should not overestimate someone's potential worth simply because of their current position in your social circle/environment. Rather, you should approach your analysis of them from as much of a blank slate as possible. If you fail to do this, you may give their cognition too much credit and find that what you thought they would process through the central route is actually being processed through the peripheral route, and vice versa. Or worse, perhaps you fail to account for the fact that certain elements of your manipulation will drive the Subject to use motivated reasoning, hot cognition, and/or heuristics in a way that you were not prepared for. Anyway, I think it is time to wrap up our discussion on societal worth and transition into the six archetypes of power. I mean, after all, this concept is sort of self-evident when you really think about it, isn't it?

SIDENOTE

Even though you should take special care not to over/under-estimate someone's potential worth, don't get too paranoid about this concept either. I say this because rules still exist, despite exceptions. In other words, someone's actual worth is still typically reflective of at least some of their potential worth and should not be discounted entirely.

So, moving on to the six archetypes of power, humans as a whole, not always, but oftentimes handle even small amounts of power over others very poorly. Well, because people are easiest to manipulate when they have the illusion of power over you, mainly because this means that they pay less attention to you and you can more easily control what information they have available to use when evaluating you, it is imperative that you understand how people change with this perceived power because, put bluntly, if you use the framework I present in this book, you will at some point be giving it to them.

To begin, unfortunately, understanding how power changes people is easier said than done, but during my research I have tried to corral all of the types of people you will see out in the real world, when they are introduced to power that is, into six stereotypes. These are the **Tyrant**, the **Martyr**, the **Cool Guy**, the **Savior**, the **Gossiper**, and the **Nerd**.

Now, here at the outset I want to implore you to keep in mind that though these archetypes are somewhat specific, these are not hard and fast rules. So, don't get too frustrated as you go through this chapter if it seems like the people that pop into your mind when hearing about these concepts regularly present with symptoms of two or more of these archetypes at the same time. The reason, even if one of these archetypes does not fit your Subject perfectly, an understanding of them as a whole will still give you a framework to identify what makes your Subject tick while also allowing you to determine the best way to persuade, deceive, or manipulate them. Anyway, now that I got that little preface out of the way, I want to lead us into this next section with another quote from Sun tzu who put it best when he said, "If you know the enemy and know yourself you need not fear the results of a hundred battles."

SIDENOTE

Even though my work has broken people down into six different archetypes, it is important to note that it is possible, and even likely that your Subject will possess traits of more than one of these archetypes. You see, humans are complex, so these archetypes exist simply to give you a framework to better understand and classify what type of Subject you will be dealing with when you give them the illusion of power over you. Not as perfect representations of them.

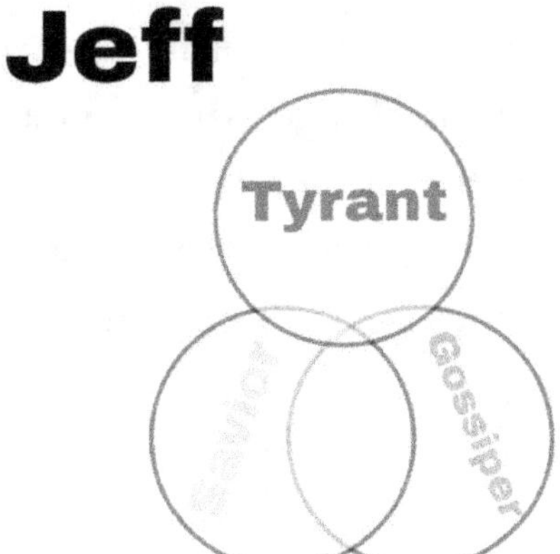

The first type of person that people become with power is an archetype that I have labeled the **Tyrant**. We have all seen these people and can probably picture them clearly at this very moment. This is because they are one of the most unpleasant of the six archetypes to be around. But be this as it may, though, luckily for us they are also by far the easiest to manipulate. You see, as I said earlier, people are easiest to manipulate when they have the illusion of power and/or authority over you. Well, the Tyrant loves power and seeks it out despite the fact they are often the worst leaders, as well as the worst stewards of authority.

Typically, the Tyrant struggles with self-esteem, self-worth, and a severe inferiority complex, and these traits often stem from their own internal recognition of their shortcomings in either intelligence or physical appearance, which subsequently make them less societally valuable. Because of these deep seated insecurities, which they attempt to hide, often times even from themselves, the Tyrant will go out of their way to impose their power on others regardless of their official title.

I saw this archetype often in the food industry, which tends to employ either ambitious young people or middle-late aged burnouts that have already "peaked." Now that may sound harsh, but it is just an unavoidable reality that very few if any 45-year-old men and women want to be flipping hamburger patties or delivering pies for minimum wage. I digress though. The Tyrant is often drawn to the food industry because it has a relatively low bar for advancement, advancement which can then be translated into power mind you, and also because it allows them to thrive even with their actual and/or perceived insecurities. I.e., this is a polite way of saying that these types of jobs are not very difficult and being good at them does not require a lot of genetic gifts.

SIDENOTE

I have worked in the food industry the entire time I have been conducting my research and going through graduate school, and I have met a lot of great people with very high potential worth during this time. So, do not look at me as some elitist fuckwad for seemingly talking a little smack. You and/or one of your friends have probably yelled at me for not getting your ranch dressing to you fast enough, and therefore I get to be blunt about this field of employment, dickhead.

Now, even though I have noticed a lot of Tyrants in the food industry, do not think for a second that they do not exist where you work as well. Putting it lightly, they are everywhere. Because of their prevalence in every industry, I think that before going further we need to stop and take a deeper look at the Tyrant because, in my view, there are actually two types of Tyrants and you need to be aware of both of them.

To begin, I found the existence of these two types of Tyrants often in my research, and therefore thought that they each deserved their own subclassification, thus making two versions of the Tyrant. These two subclassifications of the Tyrant are **"rising"** and **"faded"** Tyrants. Now it is worth noting that both of these will behave similarly, but the truth is that they do so for different reasons. In other words, even though their behavior is similar in almost every way, their underlying motivations can and likely will be slightly different from one another. To explain, the rising Tyrant has tremendous ego and believes that they are "above" whatever position they currently hold. Ergo, correcting this inward-facing feeling of not having what they deserve by advancing themselves above others is their primary motivation. Because of this the success of others will anger them, and they will seek to cut down and/or make illegitimate the accomplishments of said others while also trying to accomplish impressive things themselves.

This type of Tyrant is typically younger, more ambitious, and may therefore be more active than the faded Tyrant in their attempts to destroy and/or downplay the success of those around them. But on the other hand, though, they are often not quite as bitter as the faded Tyrant and can be reasoned with more rationally because they have not yet had to face their insecurities and come to peace with them. This means that, though they are more active and volatile, they are also not as quick to dismiss what others say just because of their own internal feelings of inadequacy. In a way, this makes them kind of like a rabid dog who is *not* cornered, and therefore is more accepting of the idea of people existing in their vicinity (they possess a stronger bite but are less likely to pounce than the other type of Tyrant).

The faded Tyrant, however, was, at least in their own mind, on the road to great things. Then, unfortunately, they got older, or at least too old for their current position in life, and the opportunity for greatness, along with hope that went with it, faded away like the memory of water in an African watering hole during the heat of the summer. Because of this they will not be content with their current position and in their minds may even believe that they did not meet their own expectations due to the success of others. This, coupled with the loss of youthful ambition and hope, will make them far more bitter and touchy than the rising Tyrant, though both are still prone to outbursts of anger that, they believe, display, and reinforce their dominance, and by proxy, relevance. Anyway, because they are bitter and unsatisfied with the levels of respect and societal status that they receive, no matter the actual amount, they will feel that they are entitled to more, and specifically, what you have, be it happiness, success, talent, or anything else that they are lacking. This outward look to others leads to a desire to eliminate the success of those around them so that they do not feel inadequate about their own failures. This is the faded Tyrants motivation. Basically, to ensure that those around them do not find success in their endeavors because this reminds them of their own failed ambitions.

SIDENOTE

In a way, because the rising Tyrant still has hope for themselves, they are generally more concerned with themselves than others. Thus why they are less likely to bite. However, the faded Tyrant has already lost hope for their future. Therefore, they are more focused on making sure everyone else fails as well. So, yes, the faded Tyrant will try to fuck with you more. Of course, with that said, they are also less ambitious and lazier than the rising Tyrant, so they will not be as effective at destroying you as the rising Tyrant, even though they are more likely to try.

To close out and summarize my description of the Tyrant, with both types of Tyrants their feelings of inadequacy, as well as their desire for more power, relevance, and control are why they need constant stimulation of their ego through instilling fear, creating perceptions of legitimacy, and achieving the illusion of control over those they see as a threat to their own self-image. This leads to them engaging in brutish, cruel, and sometimes even downright draconian behavior when they have the power to do so. They will not care about you. They will not care about your goals. And most importantly, they will have an adverse reaction to you if you are smarter than them, more attractive than them, wealthier than they are, or better than them in any other measurable way.

Now when it comes to tips on attempting to manipulate the Tyrant it is important to not come across as insincere while giving them the illusion of power over you. The reason, the Tyrant does not crave compliments, they crave respect and social status, and therefore, any half-assed attempt at using their ego and a shallow compliment to achieve this goal of giving them the illusion of power will fail because they will take it as pity, not respect. So, to give the Tyrant the illusion of power over you, you must feed their ego while also being a person whose respect they would appreciate. In other words, if you kiss too much ass you will just be seen as another insignificant fly in their presence, and at the end, they will despise you because your image will be that of a person that possesses the qualities of a minion, not a ruler, which will then remind them of their own feelings of inferiority and failure.

To avoid this pitfall, while also making sure that you do not look like a true threat (because this would engage their surveillance system and/or bad faith motivated reasoning) you must earn their respect by demonstrating some sort of value to them while at the same time posing no credible challenge to their status. Now an excellent strategy for this that I have used before is to ask them questions about something they know a lot about, or something they feel strongly about. Then, when they answer the question do not take the answer easily. Rather, propose another answer that is clearly flawed and explain passionately, but while remaining respectful, why you think your answer is actually the correct one.

Stand firm against any ad hominem attacks against your person and only after they have specifically explained why their answer is superior to yours, even if it is a bad explanation, can you concede, thus making them the superior intellect. But do not show weakness and self-deprecation when you concede defeat, though, because if you want their respect, which is a must if you are to move their latitude of acceptance through persuasion, then the Tyrant needs to see you as intelligent enough to respect, but below them enough to be one of their pawns. P.S., this is one of those rare situations wherein understanding which topics they are likely to use motivated reasoning with can be helpful.

In summary, when trying to earn the Tyrants respect while also giving them the illusion of power over you, create a disagreement and then lose; but, instead of admitting outright defeat with your tail between your legs when you lose, brush it off quickly while still giving them credit for being correct. "Oh! I get it now, thanks," then drop it. Not, "Oh my gosh, you are so smart. I can't believe I didn't see that!" If you follow this strategy, or a similar strategy whenever you feed the Tyrants ego, it allows you to maintain strength (the sender element of the SMCR) while positioning yourself "under their wisdom and tutelage," which can be very handy when you need to persuade or manipulate their attitudes and/or behaviors while using one of the routes of the elaboration likelihood model and a carefully constructed manipulative message.

The second archetype that you will see during your manipulative travels is the **Martyr**. The Martyr, unlike the Tyrant, is a leech for pity, not respect or status, and they are for the most part all the same, regardless of their age. Now, because they are after pity the Martyr may not have the energy or the will to go out of their way to explicitly fuck with you because they oftentimes are not very ambitious and simply "ended up" in a position of power (if they are in one that is). But do not expect any sympathy from them either. You see, this archetype is completely self-involved and focused only on their own life, self-image, and victimhood.

The Martyr, much like the Tyrant, will not respond well to a kiss ass. Of course, I know that this sounds counterintuitive because I just said they are a leech for pity, but to clarify; the Martyr desires pity from those around them, not unity, friendship, or a problem solver. Case in point, even as they complain the Martyr will not take responsibility for the way things are regardless of how much power they have to actually change the situation; and this means that they certainly do not want you to take responsibility when it comes to fixing their situation either. Rather, they need the suffering. Otherwise, they would have no reason to be distraught.

All of these factors suggest that the Martyr, though a serial complainer, does not necessarily want someone taking action to solve their problems, as a kiss ass would claim to want to do, but rather, they just want someone to casually engage with them about their woes, which so you can't say I didn't warn you, can be seemingly endless if you are the one having to listen. At any rate, if you ignore this warning and do end up trying to solve their problems, this will eradicate their source of pity (the problem). This will then drive them to feel anger toward you, which they will not like because this is not their motivation. No, the Martyr does not want to feel anger, they want to feel people's pity. So, if they feel anger toward you this is a deviation in their baseline and will likely lead to hot cognition and an unfavorable overall evaluation of you. Make sense?

Now for the purposes of manipulation, you should know that your Martyr will most likely be seeking pity, in some way or another, because of the "many trials" they have had to go through, not some personal flaw; and these trials generally include injustices inflicted upon them by those who hold either real or perceived power over the Martyr. If this is the case and you are dealing with a Martyr, then extended hours, budget cuts, or whatever else is the problem can all easily be blamed on those who are in a position of power over the

Martyr and yourself. And this is actually a good thing because as a result you do not have to worry about any social complications that could come from joining in with their condemnation of the perpetrators of their suffering, as you would if those perpetrators were in your immediate circle. This is because these perpetrators, the ones causing the Martyrs' suffering that is, will not be people in your immediate social circle, but rather the echelon above your social circle. I.e., if you are in a business situation, look at it like your boss (the Martyr) is the general manager of an individual branch of the company. Well, the one's causing their woes will likely be the corporate managers, and not anyone equal to them (Though sometimes they do see equals as oppressors if those equals are more dominant. In these situations you will need to be delicate and decide if the juice is worth the squeeze when it comes to the risk of causing drama in your social circle.).

But let's say that we are outside of a business situation, shall we? In non-work situations the Martyr will still always seek to place the blame for any negative outcome in their life on someone whom they believe holds power over themselves. For instance, imagine a boyfriend who blames overbearing trust issues on his mother or ex-girlfriend instead of his own insecurity; or a cheating wife who blames her infidelity on the emotional unavailability of their significant other. You see, it doesn't matter what the specific situation is (work environment or social environment), in any scenario the Martyr will seek to place themselves under someone, which, in a way, means that they need a bad guy.

All of this is to say that regardless of how the Martyr came to be where they are, they will always seek to be in the position of underdog or victim and you should take care to ensure that you are not perceived by them as being in a position of power, and also that you are not a threat to their motivation, which, if it wasn't clear before, is pity. In other words, avoid any tough love approaches that make you seem like you have authority when it comes to communicating with a Martyr because this will activate their surveillance system and either make them angry, drive them to hot cognition, or make you an actualized and tangible threat, unlike the threat of those they normally perceive as having power over them, which are generally only perceived, abstract, or even false threats that they simply use as a way to garner the pity they crave. Or put another way, make sure you do not try and fix their problems, and also that you cannot be perceived as the cause of those problems.

Continuing on with the Martyr and how to deal with them, when you recognize a Martyr, it is important that they feel you can resonate with their woes, even if you "could not possibly understand them," and that they see you as a source of pity, thus why I called them leeches by the way (they need a host's pity to thrive). In any case, making it so that they think you resonate with their situation without making them feel that you too are an equal victim can be a delicate tightrope walk, much like earning the Tyrants respect while also not threatening them. You see, simply agreeing with the Martyr about how tough they have it is not enough to feed their internal need for sympathy and pity, but on the other hand, if you resonate with them too much, they will see it as you stealing their supply of pity. Because of this conundrum I have found that the best way to empower the Martyr is to give them the opportunity to suffer in front of you. This is to say that since most of their perceived suffering is, after all, not real or just overstated, it should not be hard to find something that you can use to invoke pity. Of course, to do this, as with any manipulation, you must begin by observing the Subject and analyzing them.

During this baseline analysis stage pay special attention to what the Martyr generally uses as a source for their troubles (Often times the Martyr is lazy and goes back to the same pity trough more than once.). Then, after you have established some basic objects that they find unfavorable, you will be able to predict things that they will likely be able to enjoy focusing on. I.e., maybe it is their overbearing significant other, constant financial troubles, or an unrealistic workload. Whatever their chosen pity poison is, once you establish this aspect of your baseline analysis you can actively launch your own line of complaints and/or dissatisfaction statements regarding the parts of your shared situation or environment that you know the Martyr will agree with. In lay terms, misery loves company and the Martyr will very likely indulge in your complaints.

My advice is to keep doing this until you can link the shitty aspects you pointed out about your shared situation to the Martyr specifically. For instance, if you notice that your workplace is understaffed you could ask the Martyr when their bosses will hire more people. After they respond, comment about how much better things could be if the bosses did and mention that the understaffing sucks for you but must be even worse for people like them (the Martyr) than it is for those, like you, who do not possess leadership roles. By doing this you allow the Martyr to resonate with you without stealing their pity, which would cause them, as I said before, to see you as a threat. Furthermore, through this strategy you have inadvertently placed them above yourself ("it's worse for you") while also protecting their underdog/victim self-image; and this style of strategy will keep their negative focus off of you and instead on their abusers, while also showing that you genuinely understand/ resonate with their plight.

Alright, to wrap up the Martyr, at the end of the aforementioned example if you have a true-blue Martyr on your hands, they will not miss out on the opportunity that you presented them with, and will therefore indulge in the pity they crave. Furthermore, by putting yourself into this situation as an active catalyst for that pity, you become a conduit for pity, and a benefit of this is that from now on they will see you as somewhat valuable or even as a good and loyal soldier in their army because you help them accomplish their own personal goals of acquiring pity without making them give anything up in return, or so they think…. Anyway, this strategy of you yourself, in a way, becoming a temporary Martyr from time to time will allow you to maneuver and manipulate in their presence easily and undetected because you will not be a threat in any way. But just do not forget that when you play your Martyr card you have to give them a little something as well, otherwise you will be seen as a pity hog.

As a final note, and a personal tip, it doesn't hurt, after they have taken the reigns and made the situation about themselves that is, to let them know how sorry you are about your problems, also caused by the people above the Martyr, making their life more difficult in an already difficult time. The reason, this addition just helps ensure that they are always receiving the lion's share of the pity (bad for me, worse for you), which is something that you want if your aim is to make sure they are not using their surveillance system to cognitively process you, that they think you understand them/resonate with them, and also that they end up in a position of power over you so that you can accomplish your manipulation unnoticed and without being perceived as a threat. Good to go?

SIDENOTE

Using workplace/relationship examples is the best way to explain these archetypes. But just remember that all of these people can be anywhere, and in any position within society. I.e., I hope the examples I present make this chapter easier to understand, but your main focus should be learning the characteristics and motivations of each archetype so that you can recognize them in the unique environment you exist in.

Moving on, the third archetype I established during my research was one that I have named the **Cool Guy**. The Cool Guy is generally going to be confident and likeable because the Cool Guy, regardless of their gender, sexuality, or age does not possess a lot of internal insecurity. I.e., they are often comfortable with themselves. But as a result of this security, they can and often do lack ambition, decisive leadership skills, and/or the ability to instill discipline among their subordinates. It is because of this that they will tend to give those they see as under them quite a bit of slack. Now, even though this sounds like a good thing, it can actually make it a bit more difficult to give the Cool Guy the illusion of power, as you would easily be able to do with the Tyrant, or to make them feel like a victim, which is how you give the Martyr power. Because of this you should instead strive to give the Cool Guy the illusion of sincere admiration. The reason, gaining admiration, or being liked, is their primary motivation, and if you give it to them then this will bolster their self-image, thus inadvertently giving them the illusion of power over you without them consciously realizing it.

This admiration, though, is different from the respect the Tyrant craves or the sympathy (pity) for being "so resilient" that the Martyr craves. You see, the Tyrant, deep down sees themself as inferior and wishes to be reassured that they are in fact the opposite of this, and the Martyr actually desires to be seen as inferior to someone else, just not you. The Cool Guys, on the other hand, is confident in themselves, takes pity as an insult, and instead wishes to be liked by their subordinates. Ergo, even though they do not necessarily have anything to prove to themselves, the opinions of others still matter significantly to them and they will enjoy it when they sense admiration from these others.

Now, something to keep in mind about this archetype is that despite the nonchalant name, and the fact that they crave your admiration, Cool Guys do have a bad side. Case in point, if you get a little too loose in your manipulation and overestimate the Cool Guys "chill factor," they can quickly morph into something unrecognizable once they have been fucked over enough times. To elaborate, as I said, this archetype does not always do a good job of instilling discipline, and therefore, when they do decide to drop the discipline hammer it may be disproportional because they are correcting a lot of built up problems all at once while also not being comfortable wielding this type of power with grace and precision. So, when operating under a Cool Guy it is best to not hang yourself with the rope that they give you. Others will do this, and when they do, your stock and value to the Cool Guy will only increase as the nodes in their associative network model change to associate your competition with negative things like being late, lazy worker, and disrespectful, while the nodes associated with you are positive ones (I.e., if they are cool with people being a few minutes late, don't take advantage of this because eventually they will snap on this behavior and not be so cool about it. When that happens, anyone who has taken advantage will receive a negative evaluation.).

SIDENOTE

I am using business place and work lingo a lot in this chapter (i.e., subordinates, positions of authority, etc.). Do not be confused by this though. The workplace examples simply make explaining these concepts a bit easier. However, all of the same principles can apply to any situation. As I mentioned earlier in the chapter, there is always a dominant individual in any interaction and there are always hierarchies in social environments. Therefore, "your boss" could just as easily be a spouse, friend, relative, bandmate, professor, or any other person that you have interpersonal communications with, which again, are just manipulative dances.

Continuing on with this archetype, as I suggested before, it can be difficult to get the Cool Guy to accept being in a position of power over you. It can still be done, though, in much the same way you would tactfully gain the Tyrants' respect. This is to say that you can drive them to see you as worthy of respect, but also "not on their level." And this is important because, like the Tyrant and the Martyr, they also do not care about the admiration of insignificant kiss asses, only persons of value. Now, I won't waste time on explaining this, though, because with all of the knowledge you have thus far about choosing routes and building the best manipulation design for your specific Subject's cognition, you should be able to figure out how to earn their respect while not becoming a threat on your own (I.e., allow them to give you guidance, lose a "good faith argument, etc.). I do, however, want to talk about another unique issue manipulators have to deal with when operating under a Cool Guy. Let's move on to that now.

In addition to giving the Cool Guy the illusion of power over you, it is also difficult to manipulate a Cool Guy because in a social network consisting of more than two people, which is the majority of workplace environments, they want to be seen as fair by the highest percentage possible of those under them. Because of this, attempting to become more than a friendly acquaintance in order to manipulate them will likely lead to failure. This is because no matter how much the Cool Guy enjoys you it is not likely that they will be dishing out any special favors. So, in lieu of trying to get close to a Cool Guy, it is actually better to place distance in between you and the individual. Supply and demand are concepts that can be used in this situation.

To explain, the supply of attention the Cool Guy receives from others, which is more than likely a lot for this archetype because people end up trying to take advantage of their kindness, determines their demand for attention. So, keeping distance between yourself and the Cool Guy allows you the ability to time your overall approach and where in the timeline you place the friction point of your manipulation, which will give you the best chance at achieving success. This aforementioned strategy is very similar to a technique I have personally used to pick up a woman and one that I will share now.

While stationed in California a group of my male friends and I linked up for a weekend adventure with a group of our female friends. The ratio of men to women was two to one, so immediately we all knew that *at least* half of us were not getting laid. Given these odds, the men who were single immediately began attempting to woo the women like peacocks in mating season. I, on the other hand, knew that we had all weekend and that desperation was easily detectable. So, instead of joining the horde of horny guys, I chose to instead go off by myself with one of my buddies, and to completely ignore the women. Later the next day, when everyone was back at our condo partying, I noticed that the men were still vying for the few females' attention who were still available. Unfortunately, the poor saps, who I love and who will laugh when they read this, had spent hours throwing themselves at these ladies and made zero discernable progress.

SIDENOTE

I want to be clear that I would never in any way prey upon drunk women or do anything creepy like that. There is, however, a difference between a person being wasted and two consenting adults with a little buzz getting frisky in the sack. As we all obviously know, if people could only hook up sober, the infant care industry would go belly up. I say this only because I am talking about alcohol in this section while also talking about getting laid. I just want to get it out there that I love to party but would never cross any lines in that area. We were all adults who were having a normal and fun party. So, to all the internet deadbeats out there looking to cancel everyone, fuck off in advance.

Anyway, it was towards the end of the night, maybe 10 or 11 p.m. on that second day and I had decided that then was a perfect time to throw myself into the mix. To that end, as I scanned the party, I took notice of one woman who was being particularly flirtatious and sexual toward me. After seeing this and making eye contact with her a few more times I decided that I would hang out in her area and talk to my friend while I waited until for an opportunity to jump into her conversation with a snarky comment. The goal, after picking up on her interest in me, was to avoid hitting on her, which would have been way too direct and way too easy for her to reject, and to instead come across as uninterested in her sexually while also instigating a conversation. Put plainly, it worked, though I have to admit I don't remember the line I used, and led to her inquiring about who I was, where I was from, and all of that other shit people talk about when their subconscious minds are deciding if they want their bodies to fuck each other. I digress though. A few hours later we hit it off and banged our brains out while one of the males who had spent all day hitting on her, and who was objectively more attractive than I am I might add, sat outside angry that I had poached "his woman."

Now to bring this back to the Cool Guy, remember several things. First, when manipulating them do not be over eager. This is to say that, if possible, you should let them come to you if they want to get to know you better, not the other way around. Furthermore, if they do, do not be afraid because this is a good thing, just make sure that you keep the topics of conversation light. Second, if, on the other hand, you do have to be the one to approach them, only come to them when it is necessary for your manipulation strategy, not before. And when you do, keep in mind that they will be friendly with pretty much everyone and that most likely everyone will be friendly back. Therefore, if you are not overly nice and instead withhold your admiration at first, even if they do not consciously realize it, they will crave the admiration that you, and you alone have and control. Hell, even better, they may seek ways to actively get it by trying to figure out what they can do to earn it. This is a reaction that the other people in your environment will not get simply because they gave their admiration out too willy nilly and/or for free.

The third thing to remember about the Cool Guy is that you should not abuse their kindness by asking for favors. This is to say that people often try and take advantage of the Cool Guy by asking for special treatment and/or favors because often times it seems like there are no negative repercussions from doing so. Remember, though, that the Cool Guy seeks the admiration of all and is not likely to give special treatment. Ergo, those who seek to disrupt this status quo, after a certain amount of time, may create an association to some negative nodes within the Cool Guys associative network model. Put bluntly, you do not want to be in this boat and you do not want the Cool Guy to think of you as needy or a threat to their balance of admiration. I.e., sure, you may be able to pressure them into your demands once, and sometimes it may be a critical enough element of your manipulation to warrant it, but after this they will cease seeking your admiration and will instead see you only as a nuisance; and this will undoubtedly end any manipulation strategy you are working because now you have associated yourself, in their mind, with things that trigger their surveillance system and they will centrally process every message you throw at them, which obviously cuts your manipulative arsenal in half if you are using the principles of the elaboration likelihood model. Oh yeah, plus this moves you from the subordinate position, which ensures that they have the illusion of power over you, to a threat, which makes you more akin to an equal who doesn't respect them, and one that should be watched. Capeesh?

A fourth thing to remember, or rather an addendum to my summary of the Cool Guy that adds to the "special favors" section, is that when manipulating a Cool Guy you must create a perceived reality that gives them the desire and opportunity to bend the rules for you, but not one where you actively try and make them do so. If this sounds simple enough, just know that it can actually get very complicated, but to help explain this a little better, in essence your goal should be to create a problem that they are inspired to solve in order to gain your admiration; but, unbeknownst to them, the way in which they solve the problem is what you are really after.

In terms of getting out of work, think about it this way. You want to customize your schedule, but your boss is a Cool Guy and will not give custom schedules. If he did then he would have to for everyone. So, you need him to *want* to fix your schedule. To expand on this, if you are normally on time and a good overall employee, be late enough times that you get called into their office for disciplinary action. Then, when the topic of you being late comes up do not blame your schedule, simply focus on how busy you are with A, B, and C. Do not grovel but instead explain that you are doing your best and that you will try and find a way to move stuff around, accept full responsibility, and avoid asking for special treatment. Likely, if your classification of your boss as a Cool Guy is correct, they will offer to step in with a solution, and when they do then they have opened up the door for you to drop the friction point of your manipulation, which is that you want to set up a custom schedule.

When they bite, you can even reinforce this manipulation, to ensure that they do not get cold feet, by pretending to make only the absolutely necessary changes to get back to 100% operating output. For instance, let's say that you need Tuesdays and Wednesdays off. Your boss should think that you actually need Tuesday through Thursday off every week, but that you care so deeply about the company, your position in it, and their willingness to work with you that you will only take Tuesday and Wednesday off. In essence, this will allow you to still get the schedule you wanted while also making it seem that you are actually doing them a favor, to return their "favor," by coming in on Thursdays even though "it will make your life more difficult." In sum, this style of strategy will make them feel like a good leader, someone who is liked, and most of all, someone you admire. Just food for thought.

The fourth archetype that I established during my qualitative research study is called the **Savior**. The Savior has a very interesting motivation, which I'll talk about in a moment, but I just want to begin by saying that for the longest time I just could not pin this archetype down. In fact, during most of my research I actually thought that this archetype was so close to the Cool Guy that the Savior should not independently exist. As a result, up until recently I actually denied the Savior's existence altogether and wrote about only five archetypes (Easy Christians, I know what you are about to say. Different Savior I am denying.).

After the last 7 months of battling with myself and pondering these archetypes, however, I came to the decision that the Savior does, in fact, warrant its very own classification. You see, where I had run into problems with this archetype was in regard to the fact that, it appeared to me, the Savior did not desire power, pity, or admiration. This made the Savior, while a rather prevalent archetype, very illusive. In other words, the Savior is one of the hardest individuals to identify, and because of this I want to dedicate some time to outlining some of their features and/or giveaways.

To start, the Savior is not insecure. In fact, they tend to have many elements of a narcissist. Furthermore, they are either oblivious to their own flaws or they choose to willfully ignore them through cognitive compartmentalization. This is to say that criticisms from others will flow off of their cognition like water off a duck's ass, and thus will likely be viewed through the peripheral route or completely ignored altogether. With that said, be careful though, the Savior typically, in my research anyway, possesses an above average IQ and they will not forget about any attacks or criticisms quickly, even if they didn't actually harm their ego.

In addition to these traits, the Saviors' cunning disposition will also likely lead them to engage in outward displays of emotion similar to that of the Martyr when they are attacked or called out with the use of threatening information. And this can be very bad for a manipulator because it both draws unwanted attention and can cause others to associate your node with negative things like difficult and/or annoying. Furthermore, it will drive the Savior to see you as an overt threat, and when you interact with them, they will view anything you say as if it had come from a source/through a channel that is not credible and/or trustworthy. Good to go?

SIDENOTE

In their mind, the savior can do no wrong and any admission of guilt will likely be followed very quickly with a "but."

Alright, now that you have a brief insight into what a Savior looks like, what actually motivates the Savior? Well, according to my analyses, three words sum up their motivation perfectly.... *dedication to duty*; or, more specifically, duty to the inferior, which, ironically makes them both one of the "best" archetypes from a traditional, Western moral perspective, and also one of the easiest besides the tyrant to give the illusion of power. Anyway, you can think of this dedication to duty as an intrinsic need to be a proper "Lord" or "Lady" over those below them. You see, the Savior, though generous and kind to others, does not see them as equals. Rather, the Savior will often see them as pets or accoutrements. Accessories, if you will, to show off to their actual equals, which will likely be other Saviors whom they compete with.

Now, at the risk of sounding sexist, this also helps explain the disproportionate number of Saviors who are women. My theory as to why this is the case is that this archetype's personality construction harnesses either a deep seated maternal drive-style function, or perhaps some other form of biological mechanism centered around caretaking values, both of which are evolutionarily beneficial for women, which explains their existence. But regardless of the reason why they are the way they are, my point is that the Savior will see you as either inferior or a threat, unless you are in their inner circle, which you would obviously want to avoid if your goal is to manipulate their attitudes and behaviors through the preferred peripheral route. I digress though.

If you avoid getting close to the Savior and they view you as inferior, this can provide an excellent opportunity for you to formulate a very strong manipulation strategy. This is because you can give them the illusion of power over you and then harness their drive to be a good ruler to get them to do things that "solve" your problems, which, much like the Cool Guy they want to do, but again, for different reasons (they don't want admiration, they want to be a good superior).

Once you confirm, to the best of your ability, that you are dealing with a Savior, in many ways you have already done the hard part. I.e., sousing these people out and classifying them is harder than actually manipulating them, which is generally a surprisingly simple process. With this said, though, you still need to be cautious and must remember that a Savior, most likely, does not actually give a shit about you. So, they will not help you if it puts them at risk. This suggests that they may not even know it themselves, but they are much more focused on portraying the image of a Savior than actually saving people, which is really just a means to the end of protecting and fostering their Savior image.

Now the best way to take advantage of this, in terms of using the power structure to manipulate them that is, is to establish what I call a cub dynamic. Case in point, the Savior is always looking for someone lesser than them to use as a catalyst for their saving, and you can think of this as them wanting to be a mama (or papa) bear that wants to protect their cub. Ergo, if you want to give them the illusion of power over you and have as high of a chance of successfully manipulating them as possible, you will have to swallow some pride and become, well, to a degree, pathetic; or at least what they would consider pathetic.

Of course, when I say pathetic this does not mean whining or complaining about your situation mind you, which may work, for instance, when dealing with a Martyr. No, what this actually entails is being personally fucked up in some way or another, while also being likeable. Let me break this down.

Much like your interactions with a Cool Guy you want the Savior to want to have a desire to step in and help. With this said, though, you do not, like with a Cool Guy, want the Savior to focus on your specific problems. Rather, you want to activate their desire to fix *you* specifically. For instance, take the example from the Cool Guy section wherein you wanted a custom schedule. For the Savior you would approach this situation in much the same way as you did for the Cool Guy. This is to say that if you are a good employee and want a custom schedule, be late enough times that the boss notices. Easy day. However, the difference here is that when the Savior pulls you into their office to discuss your tardiness you should point your excuses inward. I.e., instead of talking about how you will be better and how you just have a lot going on and are having trouble keeping up, self-deprecate and talk about how you are a fuck up, have never been good at this type of stuff, and really want to do a good job but just don't know how. The reason, this will give the Savior a perfect opportunity to accept power over you and step in to correct your flaws. Likely, if you do a good enough job guiding them in this direction and have also been an otherwise good employee, they will do this through the implementation of a custom schedule that *you* can handle.

SIDENOTE

Unlike the Cool Guy, giving preferential treatment will not be a problem for the Savior, so long as you do not resort to the previous behavior of being late once the manipulation is complete. The reason I say this is because even though you can garner specific requests from the Savior, you must make them feel as if they truly did fix you. Otherwise they will subconsciously see you as a threat because you are now actively working against their ultimate motivation, being a good ruler who takes care of their Subjects (and improves them).

Ok, we are almost at the end folks, so stay with me. The last two archetypes I established during my research were the Gossiper and the Nerd. To keep things moving along smoothly we will start with the Gossiper because this is one of the archetypes that I saw with disproportionate frequency when I was studying the ways in which people change when they receive power.

To begin, the **Gossiper** is interesting because they do not seek power in the traditional sense. This is to say that, unlike the Tyrant, they do not necessarily want official control over anyone. Instead, the source of their power, as well as their motivation, is in the name, gossip. Now for clarity, gossip is essentially just using communication to intentionally exploit aspects of another person's social image in order to manipulate how others see that person or their contributions to the social environment, which is very likely going to sew a degree of chaos. The end goal of engaging in this behavior, interestingly enough, though, is not to elevate the Gossiper's own status by breaking down another's social image. Rather, it is almost solely about using gossip to catalyze the release of the adrenaline and endorphins that the Gossiper gets through the process of creating social chaos, which does inherently bring with it the breaking down of one or more other individual's social images, but again, is not the ultimate goal.

Because these types of people are typically ones that exhibit elements of narcissism and/or sociopathy, wherever they are they will enjoy, and likely even thrive amidst interpersonal conflict and as a result may even conjure it out of nowhere. So, if you are just thinking about a bunch of bored housewives pounding screw top wine and talking about Jennifer's divorce; instead, I want you to imagine a politician blackmailing a member of their own party or a coworker talking shit about another coworker to the boss when they have nothing to gain.

The existence of these types of scenarios, which I saw more than one would think during my research, suggests that the Gossiper can be any gender, in any profession, and as a result may completely surprise a manipulator if that manipulator has not noticed them and categorized them. I digress though. In addition to all of this, Gossiper's are also master deflectors and will typically seek to redirect any criticisms of themselves with the purpose of creating social divides among those around them. And the Gossiper is also a natural talent when it comes to finding ways to disrupt the social order, and as a result, they often accidentally manipulate themselves into positions of power by alienating their competition and will do this without any help from you.

This means that you will probably not have to try very hard to give the Gossiper the illusion of power over you and/or make yourself seem inferior to them in terms of worth. I.e., as a byproduct of their nature they will destroy everyone around them, thus resulting in them raising their social status within your environment by comparison. But it also means that you should be very cautious when it comes to engaging with the Gossiper, in particular before they have power, because the way they gain power is often by incidentally damaging the social stock of their competition, which could be you or anyone else close to them in the social environment who poses a threat.

Now after that last sentence this may sound counterintuitive to say, but when dealing with a Gossiper you cannot always wait for them to come to you like you would try to do with the Cool Guy and the Savior. However, approaching them is also tricky because you cannot be too aggressive when trying to get their attention. You see, a Gossiper craves the entertainment that comes with their sewing of chaos and if you are an active part of their cognition, which you should try to avoid for the most part but is something that cannot always be helped, and you refuse to give it to them, they will probably make you an enemy of someone else in order to satiate their desires.

At any rate, due to the volatility of this archetype, to avoid being the catalyst for their gossip what you have to do is make them feel like you are not a threat while also giving them a sacrificial lamb; and you can achieve this by establishing a common enemy and engaging in the act of gossiping yourself. Of course, this part can get messy considering that the enemy will have to be someone you know in common, so my advice is to pick someone who you either can afford to lose as an ally or someone who cannot harm you in the future should they discover your manipulation. In other words, someone whose potential and actual worth you have correctly accessed and someone whom you have determined is not a threat to your plans, should they find out about your gossip. Anyway, when establishing your common enemy you do not have to go overboard, but you *do* need to show discernable dissatisfaction and/or frustration about this common enemy, at least when you are around the Gossiper that is.

In lay terms, do not be overtly obvious. Instead, just be visible enough to let the Gossipers drama radar go off. Perhaps this is just a passing comment in the break room or maybe it is making eye contact with them and feigning annoyance with an eyeroll after you notice that they have been observing you interact with the aforementioned common enemy. However you choose to do it, if they do not approach you, continue escalating or switch to someone else that you know the Gossiper is not favorable toward. Why, you ask? Eventually, if you have a Gossiper on your hands, they will bite.

When they do, this is the first step, and it is a big one at that, but do not get overly excited and instead ensure that you do not be selfish with the gossip. This is to say that, sure, join them in discussing your shared views of the common enemy, but allow them to do the heavy lifting. This not only makes them feel that they are the puppet master, but it will also make them see you as a person they can approach and vent to in the future. Furthermore, it associates you, in their associative network model, with positive things. This is because you have, through the alienation of the common enemy, made yourself a safe source of gossip that they can go to when they need a fix. But just be careful that you don't give them too much at once because when you start feeding the Gossiper they will expect the same portion each time. So, my advice is to only interact with them when it is necessary to advance your manipulation because this keeps the amount of collateral social damage to a minimum. I.e., since you need to direct their attention to someone else, and that other person may not like the fact they are getting gossiped about, you want to make sure you only do this when necessary. Otherwise, you will burn too many bridges too fast.

SIDENOTE

This chapter covers the archetypes of power, how to give them the illusion of power over *you* specifically, and also how to avoid activating their surveillance systems. If you are wondering what to do once they have the illusion of power over you, well, use the other concepts and principles in this book to establish a more thorough baseline of them and then formulate a manipulation strategy that is specifically designed for their baseline/archetype, and one that accomplishes your specific goals. But what's that, you say? You have already given them the illusion of power over you but you don't yet have a manipulation planned? Well, that was a dumb move on your part to approach them then.

Remember, you only want to approach a Subject when you want to manipulate them and/or lay the groundwork for a manipulation. So, do not go through all of this and do not give them the illusion of power over you until you have a plan for using this new position. Otherwise, you have just started the process without having a discernable plan or overall goal, which, in the case of the Gossiper, means that you have unnecessarily made a mess of your social environment and added risk to your overall manipulation for no reason.

Alright, to wrap up this archetype, the Gossiper requires a lot of maintenance due to their personality traits, one of which is a short attention span. Because of this you must be very careful when you find one. This is to say that in the early stages, when observing the

Gossiper and learning their baseline, you should not let your guard down. Now this may seem obvious, but to reiterate, the Gossiper is not explicitly after the destruction of others. They simply want the release that comes from creating social chaos, and they can do this with you or without you, it makes no difference to them.

And to add to this, also remember that, once you have made contact, the Gossiper will just as easily turn on you. So, the less they know about you and the less you personally interact with them the better, especially early on; but even after you have approached them, remain somewhat uninteresting so that your only connection to them is being an outlet for what they crave, gossip, and not someone who could make an interesting target (if they know you are getting a divorce, a hardcore supporter of an unpopular political candidate, etc., they can use this info against you).

Ok everyone, this next archetype is the last one and will be the one with the shortest explanation, so hang in there. The final archetype I want to discuss is, in many ways, the opposite of the Gossiper, and this final archetype is the **Nerd.**

This type of person, at least in terms of when they are introduced to real or perceived power, has been partially recognized already by American culture in the past. This is to say that people have had names for it long before I came along with this book. Teacher's pet, kill joy, and type-A are just some of these names and they all describe this type of person perfectly. You see, the Nerd values and craves order, punctuality, and efficiency. This is, in a way, their motivation, perfection.

To that end, the Nerd is by the book and will not value admiration, gossip, or personal praise, only results. They are clinical and will see you only in terms of what you provide to the overall in-group, be it a company, family, or a class of students. Furthermore, as a result of their natural cognitive disposition and personality traits, logic and the central route will likely be the best persuasive strategy to use on the Nerd. This is because they will more than likely not react to emotional appeals and you will instead have to manipulate them by using reason and sound arguments. Of course, needless to say, this can become extremely difficult when trying to use deception and misdirection, however, if you use a combination of level-one and level-three lies, which we cover in the next chapter, it is possible. Just remember, though, that the Nerd is one of if not the most difficult archetypes to manipulate and one of the least forgiving if a manipulation is discovered. So, proceed with extreme caution!

SIDENOTE

Much like the Savior and the Gossiper, giving the Nerd the illusion of power is very easy. In fact, it is very likely that you will not have to do anything at all in order to achieve this. You see, the Nerd typically has a high IQ and a propensity for leadership, and with these two things comes either quiet confidence, or implicit arrogance. So, as long as you avoiding becoming a threat, the Nerd, if that is truly the correct classification of the individual, will take care of putting themselves in a position of power over you all on their own. This is because they typically rise to the top of whatever field they are in; or at the very least, they have the attention of and sway over the individuals who do have power, at least enough that it makes them feel as if they are in a position of authority themselves. Ergo, just like a teacher's pet has more sway (inter-classroom political power) than the average student, a Nerd who doesn't have actual status can still be quite powerful.

Moving on, despite the inherent difficulties that come with manipulating someone who will not initially rely on heuristics or other forms of cognitive shortcuts, there are still a few ways that you can set yourself up for the successful manipulation of one. To elaborate, because of their dedication to order, ensure that when you are dealing with a Nerd that you avoid being inconsistent. The reason, reliability is going to be a node you want associated with your name in the Nerds associative network model; and furthermore, you must be reliable in order to earn their respect, which is important because if they respect you then they will trust you and trust is going to be crucial when dealing with the Nerd because the only time a Nerd would even think about using the peripheral route and/or low levels of evaluation around you is if they trust you.

Of course, it deserves mention, though, that earning the Tyrant and the Cool guy's respect is different from earning the Nerds respect. I.e., when it comes to the Nerd, this respect and trust building stage is the most difficult part of the manipulation and requires both time and productivity on your part because, unlike those other two archetypes, the Nerd respects only those who *actually perform* in measurable and quantifiable ways. This is to say that they will not respect anything other than you producing results, whatever that may mean in your specific situation (i.e., maybe this is being a good spouse instead of being a productive employee.) Good to go?

When it comes to power, the Nerd is anal enough and intelligent enough that they know when they are in a position of power and when they are not, so this will be essentially a non-factor to you as long as you do not outperform them. With this in mind, your goal should simply be to avoid becoming a threat, which you can do by being consistent, and also by limiting how many times you do whatever their version of a fuck up is. Furthermore, you should also take care to, as stated before, earn their trust because after it is earned, which again can be easier said than done, you can begin to alter their attitudes and behaviors by using their central processing and misdirection. In other words, you get them to a place where, when your arguments look logical on their face, they do not feel the need to inspect your communications closely enough to find a reason to challenge them because you have a proven track record.

Now, full disclosure, if all of this sounds like a lot, it should. Put plainly, with the Nerd manipulations will take longer because you have to move slow in order to avoid mixing up your narratives, avoid getting caught in a deception or misdirection attempt, and avoid having an attempt to sabotage someone else blow up in your face. Also, you have to ensure that the sender, message, and channel factors of your manipulation are perfectly structured. Despite these intimidating considerations, though, and the fact that the Nerd is by far the most difficult and time consuming archetype to manipulate, manipulations of the Nerd are very possible. And as a bonus, these manipulations typically involve people who have a high potential worth (as mentioned in the margin sidenote Nerds often have high IQ's) which makes them, yes, time intensive, but also well worth it. Just do not forget that the Nerd, although a valuable ally, once you gain their favor that is, is a horrendous enemy who is not likely to change a negative evaluation of you once it is made. Anyway, to close this out, when manipulating a Nerd be prepared to put in an immense amount of "honest work" to garner their trust, and then prepare for an even slower tight rope walk when it comes to adjusting their latitude of acceptance through the central route of persuasion.

Ok, that is it for this chapter my friends. Before we get out of here, though, I just want to leave you with a quick endnote to tie it off neatly since this was, after all, the longest chapter. Sound good? Great, then without further to do, when you learn to identify people's potential worth and how they handle power you will be able to recognize who is a threat and who is not, who has weak points in their cognition and/or personality traits that you can use and leverage when you are developing strategies for your manipulations, and also how to best present yourself so that you are not yourself seen as a threat by your Subject, but rather as a source for whatever their motivation is. But with this said, each individual person and situation is different and many will not fit every archetype or pattern precisely. This means that you, as the architect of your own reality and the perceived realities of those around you, will have to adapt and, for lack of a better phrase, prepare for the unexpected by giving yourself wiggle room in your manipulation planning. Put another way, in the Marine Corps we have a saying that goes, "No plan survives first contact." Frankly, this is true for manipulation as well, and regardless of how well you get at behavioral prediction you should expect parts of your strategy to fail or encounter resistance. Because of this you should use these archetypes as a reference and/or framework to help you learn the baseline behavior and motivations of your Subjects; but you should also be careful to not get too reliant on them as a tool that you can use to neatly box in your Subjects. If you do, then you will undoubtedly be surprised by aspects of their behaviors and/or attitudes that do not jive with the archetype and baseline you have attributed to them. Make sense?

As one final note, this book is also, though to a lesser degree if I am being honest, written for people struggling with being manipulated themselves. Well, if you are trying to avoid being manipulated and are not finding success……. reassess the power structures in your life and then ask yourself, "Which one of these Archetypes best describes me?" Ok everyone, see you in the next chapter wherein we will be discussing the four dimensions of lying.

What is Lying

I'm not upset that you lied to me,
I'm upset that from now on I can't believe you. **—Nietzsche**

Well fuck me. That last chapter was a mouthful, wasn't it? I suppose my plan of making these chapters short is not panning out as I had hoped. Oh well. I still think that it is worth it because all of these chapters cover important parts of the communication landscape and the overall manipulation process as a whole. But with that said, we are finally to the topic that inspired this entire work. That is, why do some lies succeed whereas others fail? Pretty exciting, yeah?

Before conducting my research, this question was one that I had wrestled with for a long time, especially after noticing the fact that during my time in the military the exact same lie may completely fail in one circumstance only to overwhelmingly succeed in another. Because of this problem, which is what you would actually call it from a researcher's perspective, I began to study what makes one lie

211

either successful or unsuccessful; and after years of research, and a quantitative experiment that I allude to often during this chapter, my studies finally yielded an answer. This answer, which I have empirically tested, is what I will share here. In essence, it is a 4-dimensional model of lying wherein the success or failure of each lie, as well as where it exists in this model, is dependent upon certain internal elements, and how external factors influence and/or change these internal elements.

Now, the reason this work is so important to you reading and/or listening to this is because, as you no doubt already know, manipulation quite often requires the use of deception. In fact, in some way or another pretty much every manipulation you conduct or souse out during your travels will have the element of deception in it. Because of this, I feel that my work, and this book in particular, would not be complete without a thorough review of what makes a good deception, what makes a bad deception, and also how this 4-dimensional system can be applied to ensure that your manipulations are as full-proof as possible. To that end, this understanding of deception is especially important during the friction point of any manipulation, but it is also important when it comes to how you lay the groundwork for a manipulation. Of course, you don't need to get too worried about this right now because it goes without saying that this will be explained better in the following pages, so for now just know that deception is a major part of manipulation and that there are certain "hard" rules that you can utilize when using it. Good to go? Great, then let's embark into the chapter, which I want to begin by outlining some noteworthy technical elements of the quantitative study I conducted to test my hypotheses.

Research question: What makes a lie either successful or unsuccessful?

Theory: Lies can be broken down into 4 categories. I believe that levels 1 and 3 will have a significantly higher success rate than levels 2 and 4.

Model: A successful lie = Pattern + Face Value Believability + Baseline + Friction Points + Lines of Verifiability

Hypotheses:

H_1- I believe that level 1 and 3 lies, used together or separately, will be more successful than level 2 and 4 lies.

H_2- fewer children, lower age, and more prominent religious beliefs will correlate with higher levels of lie success.

H_0- There will be no significant difference between the levels of lies.

To start, if you remember chapter one then you remember that when we are communicating with each other we are telling stories, and it does not matter if what you are saying is true or false, you are telling a story, nonetheless. Ergo, fact or fiction aside, when communicating you are creating a narrative that conveys something that influences the individual on the other end; and it is worth noting that these communications do not have to be particularly lengthy or detailed, even though this is what we think of when we think of storytelling. Put another way, even mundane bits of information are, in a way, still a story.

To illustrate, do you remember the example I gave of this in the second chapter? If not, the example I used was me telling my roommate, "I placed a gallon of milk in the refrigerator." In this scenario my roommate can easily visualize me doing this. Therefore, whether I did or didn't is kind of irrelevant at the current moment because in their perceived reality they have access to milk and will think/behave accordingly. And in addition to this, remember that if they believe me, simply saying "Yes" when they ask me if I got milk is the same as if I had told them a lengthy diatribe about how I had hunted and killed a mighty dragon named Basi in order to get the milk. In fact, the only true difference between these two stories is that one is more likely to be believed than the other (Which is where this system of classifying lies can help you quite a bit I might add.).

You see, by replying yes, even though it is only one word, I have used deception to alter my roommate's perceived reality and the world in which he now exists. Of course, if you now remember the example fully, when he goes to the kitchen and there is no milk to be found my false story will fall apart and the landscape of our lives will change direction. However, until the climax of this friction point, he has a fridge full of milk and will operate accordingly based on this premise. Sound familiar?

Alright, moving on, to loosely parrot something that I said in an earlier chapter again, *if communication is just a form of storytelling, and if we communicate for self-serving purposes, then it stands to reason communication at its very nature is an act of manipulation wherein we are trying to alter the attitudes or behaviors of those around us. So, communication it seems, assuming this premise is correct, is a constant pushing and pulling of curated fact and fiction between two or more parties. Furthermore, if we are motivated by self-serving desires, as previously discussed, there will remain a constant competition of momentum, like the tides of the ocean against a cliff, with one person always maintaining the dominant position during any communication session. What I mean by this is that there is purpose to the stories we tell, regardless of length, and they are designed to do something for us. From telling a story to get your way out of a speeding ticket to giving your girlfriend a compliment to make her smile, your stories have purpose. Now, much of our communication is obviously dull and inconsequential so in this book I am focusing mostly on the false stories we share. To make things simple I will just use the word lies. Do not forget, though, that lies are just false stories with a manipulative, self-serving purpose, regardless of "good" or "bad" intent.* Again, sound familiar?

Bringing this quotation back to my research for this chapter, after understanding the true nature of communication and what a lie truly is, I became even more curious about the success of some people when it came to pulling off seemingly preposterous lies while others could not successfully convince a person of even a mundane lie. I mean, even as far back as my high school days I realized through observing those around me that there was a delicate balance between success and failure when it came to lies, and also that some simple lies, like whether milk is in the fridge or not, can be unbelievable while farfetched tales, like that I was not really kissing Sarah Buscemi behind my girlfriends back even though multiple witnesses had seen me, seemed to be accepted hook line and sinker. I digress though. This state of affairs not only perplexed me but also fascinated me at the same time, and that fascination led me to the research question, theory, and hypotheses listed at the beginning of this chapter. And at the end of trying to understand these queries I was left with results that, among other things, have helped me figure out why the milk story, which is a real example, failed, and why the story about my girlfriend, which is also true, did not.

Anyway, now that you are refreshed about what a lie actually is and why they interested me in the first place, I want to share with you how to classify them. To do this I will be using the real examples that I used during my experiment, which consisted of a representative sample of over 300 Phoenix residents, as well as a few that were not a part of that study. Sound like a plan? Great.

SIDENOTE

I will explain each of these levels in detail, but to start, these are the elements of a level-one lie.

Level 1

1) The lie creates only a mild disruption in the baseline (It is plausible given the context of the environment, it is not a novel issue that draws unusual interest, etc.).

2) The lie must have a direct line of verifiability between the teller and receiver (i.e., you could say you caught the flu on the train, but not through a mutual friend).

3) The lie contains only one source of friction (for instance, X+B+H= my inability to attend your event contains three sources of friction.).

4) Within the baseline, it is slightly more reasonable that the lie is true than that teller would lie (i.e., why would a good employee lie about his car being in the shop).

5) The lie is not representative of a disruptive pattern.

Level-one lies, or as I have nicknamed them, menial stories, are false narratives that deviate from the baseline slightly, but not so much that they arouse suspicion, and in a way, these already have a name. That name is a white lie. You see, a white lie generally references a lie that has the intent of achieving a desired outcome, but not one that intends to do significant harm. For instance, when your wife has put on a few pounds and asks if she looks chunky, you obviously, unless you are a real dick, will tell her the white lie that she looks thin and fit because you are seeking to protect her feelings.

Because of this common correlation with *good* and/or *nice* things, white lies are generally acceptable within society, and people see them as inconsequential to the overall narrative of life. A level-one lie, or menial story is much broader than this, though, because the self-serving root is the same as any other level of lie. This is to say that the goal and intent of the lies make no difference in the context of communication as a whole. Case in point, whether it is a menial story to get out of going to a friend's destination wedding or to protect someone's feelings (like your chunky wife), the level of lie has not changed, regardless of the motivation, and we use this level of deception almost instinctively. In fact, many of them pass unnoticed by either willful ignorance or a lack of interest by the person being told the lie, and this suggests that there is sometimes an element of cognitive dissonance that comes with these lies. But let's not get into a rabbit hole about that here.

This level of deception is very easy to get away with if the teller can remain calm and casual so as to not arouse suspicion. However, even if the Subject is not an FBI or CIA analyst who has extensive experience with interrogations, most people may be able to detect these lies by plugging them into the narrative you are spinning as a whole and seeing if they fit. The reason, these little lies are often when people make mistakes, such as contradicting themselves or mixing up dates and times. Ergo, it is important to not disregard level-one lies as silly little throwaway tales that you do not have to properly structure because even though the average person will not be an agent specifically trained in sniffing out deception, nonetheless, this skill is natural to all humans, and therefore, it is to be expected that Subjects of a level-one lie may have follow-up questions. This is why it is important to, for lack of a better phrase, cover your bases, which brings us to the elements of a level-one lie, all of which you need to know in order to ensure your level-one deception has a sturdy foundation.

As mentioned before, level-one lies do not deviate from the baseline enough to cause a significant disruption. Now, from the chapter on baselines you should have a pretty good understanding of what this means, but put plainly, a lie can only be a level-one lie if it is a likely possibility that it is true within your environment. In other words, if you do not have a car and your manipulation involves car trouble, this would create a rather significant disruption because, well, now you have to explain how you got a car, when you got it, why the Subject did not know about it, etc.

The second element of a level-one lie is that it must have a direct line of verifiability between the sender and receiver. This means that a level-one lie must have only one accessible source, you. To illustrate, imagine you tell your Subject that you caught the flu. If you say you got it from a stranger on the train, then there is only one person that Subject can go to in order to verify your story. You. But if you said you got the flu from one of your coworkers, on the other hand, now you have given your Subject the ability to check your story with someone else. Now maybe this person does have the flu and confirms that they gave it to you, but if this is not confirmed beforehand (if they won't lie for you) the risk is too great for that lie to be a level-one lie.

The third element of a level-one lie is that there is only one friction point. In lay terms, this means that there is only one reason for the existence of your lie. To elaborate, if you have a car and you were telling a lie about car trouble, the reason (friction point) could be that your alternator is bad, not that your alternator went out, your bus ran late, and then you hurt your ankle and couldn't make it to the next stop in time. Of course, this can seem a bit counterintuitive because we have been told that the more detailed a lie the more likely it is to be believed, but the truth of the matter is that multiple friction points raise suspicion and also create innumerable possibilities for you to, well, fuck up. So, keep it simple stupid (KISS method).

The fourth element of a level-one lie is similar to the first, but not exactly so. Basically, a level-one lie must be believable within your baseline of behavior. Or put another way, if you are a good employee who has a record of being honest then it is believable that you are telling the truth about not being able to make it when you call off. If you are a bad employee who lies a lot, though, then your Subject will not trust you as much, since your baseline is negative, and this lie will likely not be believed without evidence (real or fabricated). So, be mindful of your reputation.

The fifth and final element of a level-one lie is that it must not be a part of a disruptive pattern. To use the car example again, if you were always using your alternator as a friction point, then this is no good. You see, disruptive patterns can be good for laying the groundwork of a manipulation, but not for creating believable friction points. In other words, you could lay the groundwork for your alternator going out by reinforcing the fact that your car is a piece of shit, but not by specifically telling everyone your alternator is faulty because this second option would make the lie familiar in their minds, and as previously mentioned, will arouse suspicion (I.e., why does he keep bringing this up and not doing something about it?). And furthermore, it will remove the potency of your lie because you have, essentially, "worn out" that node connection within their associative network model, and when you use the alternator story it will not be as unique to your Subject, and therefore, they will not be as kind or supportive as they would be if it had been a surprise to them that came from a non-threatening source.

SIDENOTE

During my experiment this is the preamble I included before the situations I presented,

"For the following scenarios please select the answer that comes closest to your initial gut reaction. In each scenario, the person is either lying or telling the truth. There is no pattern. All could be lying, all could be telling the truth, or it could be a randomized mixture. Simply try and answer as honestly as possible for each situation."

I wanted to show you this now so that you can better understand the situations I present throughout the rest of the chapter.

P.S. After each scenario the participants could choose between four options. I believe them, I mostly believe them, I mostly do not believe them, and I do not believe them.

To show you how this breaks down in practice I will use an example of a level-one lie from my experimental study. That example is as follows:

A pizza delivery driver calls out of work 50 minutes before their shift. They tell the manager that their vehicle is not starting and that they will not be able to work their scheduled shift. The driver owns a 2013 Toyota corolla that appears to be in average condition. The driver called off one time earlier this year due to vehicle issues. This was 8 months ago. They did not provide any documentation.

In this example, it is highly likely that the driver will be believed. This is because it meets all of the requirements of a level-one lie. First, given the context of a pizza parlor, which will typically employ low to low-middle socioeconomic class employees, it is not strange to have a delivery driver call off due to car trouble. So, this lie will only create a small disruption in the baseline of the pizza parlors' environment. Second, the lie has only one line of verifiability because the only person that the manager of the pizza parlor can rely on for situation-relevant information is, in fact, the employee. Third, this lie contains only one friction point, which is car trouble. Fourth, it is more likely, given the baseline of the driver who had only called off once in recent history due to car trouble, that the employee is truly having car trouble than that they are coming up with a random lie. And the fifth and final element that makes this lie a level-one lie is that this lie does not represent a disruptive pattern. I.e., as mentioned, in the scenario the driver has only called off once this year and that was 8 months ago. Therefore, there is no explicit reason to suspect their story of being a lie due to frequency of use.

As you can see, all of the individual elements of a level-one lie generally work together. This is to say that things like avoiding a lie that creates a disruptive pattern in the baseline will ensure that it does not raise suspicion, which in turn keeps it from drastically disrupting the baseline of your behavior. Furthermore, by making only one friction point the employee is able to control the lines of verifiability. If instead, though, the employee added in that they could not get anyone else from work to pick up the phone, presumably so that they could ask them to borrow their car, well, then the manager or store owner could reach out to the individuals that the employee had claimed to try and reach; and if the employee had not actually tried to contact these other employees, then there would be multiple lines of verifiability, due to this extra friction point, and the overall manipulation could come tumbling down like a house of cards. Make sense? Great, then to close out our discussion of level one lies, make sure you do not overlook any of the elements because they all work together and support one another.

SIDENOTE

You may notice that the elements of level-two and level-four lies have a lot of latitude and/or wiggle room. The reason for this is that level-one and level-three lies are "good" lies in the sense that they are the lies most likely to be believed. Therefore, they have some very strict requirements. Level-two and level-four lies, however, are "bad" lies in the sense that they are not very likely to be believed. And they are also more common. So, because level-two and level-four lies represent a far greater number of lies than level-one and level-three lies do, mainly because people are bad liars even despite doing it so much, the standards to classify a lie as level-two or level-four must be less strict since, in essence, these levels have to contain all of the lies that are not "good" lies. I just wanted to clarify this before getting too deep into the weeds because you are certainly going to notice that I am a lot broader when speaking about level-two and level-four lies.

The next dimension of lying, as you may suspect, is level-two lies. I like to think about level-two lies as lies that are somewhat reasonable lies but also ones that deviate from the baseline just far enough that they warrant moderate levels of suspicion. In other words, these lies,

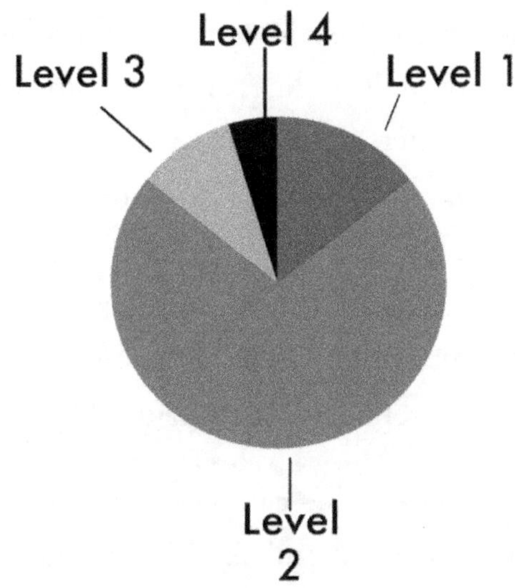

unlike level-one lies, do not make it easy for the receiver to ignore them and instead force the listener to determine which is more likely, that the person is lying, or that their story is true; and this is a bad thing for manipulators because level-two lies are not an extreme deviation from the baseline, but they are still unlikely. This is to say that with a level-two lie it is, at face value, more likely that you are lying than that you are telling the truth.

The fact that it is, at face value, more likely that these lies are false than that they are true contributes to why these lies are the number one type of lie that gets people caught. Basically, these lies are typically born from nervousness, panic, or just overall carelessness and leave too many openings within them for the receiver to find flaws. Anyway, the elements of a level-two lie are as follows:

Level 2

1) The lie creates a moderate disruption in the baseline (it is excessive given the context of the environment).

2) The lie can have a direct line of verifiability between the teller and receiver, or multiple lines of verifiability between the teller, receiver, and others.

3) The lie can have one source of friction or many.

4) Within the baseline, it is slightly unreasonable to assume that the teller is telling the truth (i.e., this is the third time this month that the employee has been "sick").

5) The lie may be reflective of a disruptive pattern.

As you can see level-two lies can be very similar to level-one lies, however, a level-two lie will be missing one or more of the elements of a level-one lie. Now this may not seem like much, but given the delicacy required to pull off a truly masterful deception, whatever element is missing is going to be a big deal, especially because all the elements work together. Of course, with that said, a level-two lie still may work, but it is quantifiably less likely. At any rate, let's look at another example that I used in my experiment to go through each element of a level-two lie and discuss how these lies are different from a level-one lie. That situation is as follows:

An individual calls their significant other and says they have to work late again, and that they should not wait up. This is the 12th time in 2 months the partner has had to work late, and the couple has had intimacy issues since it started. The partner who is working late took this job and has been happy with it because, historically, it has been a low-stress job with relaxed hours. The partner never had to work late for the 3 years leading up to this recent change.

Right off the bat we can see that there has been a "more than slight" deviation in the baseline. To elaborate, not only has the baseline of the job (hours worked) changed and experienced a deviation, but so too has the baseline of the individual's libido and/or the couple's sex life (intimacy issues). These deviations in the baseline are not subtle things, and therefore, when combined warrant a heightened level of scrutiny from the receiver of the deception. In short, these deviations in the baseline are likely going to cause a lot of disruption in the normal routine of the couple's life, and by proxy, will arouse a lot of suspicion from the receiver.

Continuing to go down the list of elements for a level-two lie, let's look at lines of verifiability. Remember that a level-two lie can have just one line of verifiability, or many. Well, in this case, the disruption of the baseline alone would be enough to disqualify the lie the individual told from being a level-one or level-three lie; however, this situation also contains more than one line of verifiability because the significant other knows where the individual works. Because of this, they could reach out to the individual's coworkers, supervisors, or even just the main office line. So, with this in mind, even if the lie created only a mild disruption in the baseline, which it doesn't, it still could not be considered a level-one lie because level-one lies require the lie to have only one line of verifiability.

Now, while we are on the topic of verifiability, I might as well note that multiple lines of verifiability could also become multiple friction points. Of course, if the significant other does not use these supplementary lines of verifiability (does not reach out to the significant other's work contacts), then this will not be the case; but nonetheless I would not feel comfortable having that door open and available for the Subject of the manipulation to use, should they get suspicious. In any case, with that said, let's move on and examine the baseline elements.

When it comes to the baseline, level-two lies make it difficult for the receiver of the lie to just accept it at face value. Well, since this element ties directly into the baseline disruption element, which we have already talked about, I would just say that I think it is obvious how this lie would look whilst judging it at face value (i.e., one plus one is two and the likelihood that the work hours and libido are not connected is unlikely.). And last but not least, in this scenario the individual displayed a pattern of actions that were disruptive to the baseline. I mean, yes, abnormalities in the baseline are generally bad for manipulators because they arouse suspicion, so I can see how one would think that this disruptive pattern, because it was a pattern, was a good thing, especially for a person trying to lay the groundwork for a specific manipulation; however, this is not correct because the pattern is not a pattern of unsuspicious behavior. Rather, it is a pattern of disruptive behavior, as far as the baseline is concerned anyway, and the amalgamation of these individual data points in the pattern raises suspicion greatly over time. Furthermore, as we already know, a person with heightened suspicion will be using their what, that's right, surveillance system. So, yeah, a disruptive pattern of this nature would do more damage than good (they will likely think you are untrustworthy, not that you are just innocently discombobulated).

Anyway, to wrap this section up a level-two lie can take on a lot of different forms. Now, you do not have to know all of these variations, but rather just that, even if a lie is not extremely abnormal, which would indicate a level-four lie, if it does not meet even just one the requirements of a level-one or level-three lie, then it is a bad lie.

SIDENOTE

Ok, we are halfway through the chapter folks so I hope you are still following me, but either way I am moving on.

A level 3 lie, in my opinion, is the perfect type of lie, and it is profoundly effective. This being said, though, the downside of the level 3 lie is that it cannot be used more than once, and the reason for this is that this level of lie is, essentially, a lie that deviates from the baseline so profoundly that the chances the sender made it up are less than the absurdity of the lie itself. In other words, these lies are so far out of the baseline that they, in a way, shock the listener. Of course, with that said, they do, however, still remain within the realm of reality given the specific baseline of the environment, sender, and receiver. So, don't get them confused with the absurdity of a level-four lie, which we will get to in a bit.

You see, individuals in modern societies typically want to assume the best about people, despite the fact that most people are naturally skeptical of their fellow man or woman. Well, if you can capitalize upon this, you can basically provide yourself with a nuclear option type of lie. Now, we will get into how to actually set up these lies (with level-one lies) in a bit, but for now let's just start by looking at the elements of a level-three lie, as well as another example I used during my experiment, in order to gain a better understanding of these types of false stories. Sound good? Sweet, then without further to do, as always, the elements of a level-three lie are as follows:

Level 3

1) The lie creates a significant disruption in the baseline.

2) The lie has one or multiple lines of substantive verifiability (i.e., documentation, witness testimony, credible alibi, etc.)

3) The lie can have more than one source of friction but each must have at least one line of verifiability (layered cause).

4) The lie disrupts the baseline to such a degree that, at face value, it seems more reasonable that the lie is true than that the teller simply "came up with it."

5) The lie is not representative of a disruptive pattern.

The situation we will use to explain how these work in practice is as follows:

The organizer of a local charity that delivers food on weekends hears their phone ring. One of their paid section managers calls to tell them that they can't make their manager shift, which starts in two hours. They tell the organizer that their roommate borrowed their car. The roommate was rear-ended at a stop light and their car was towed to the shop. They will not be able to do managerial work for a few days. They tell the organizer they can provide documentation if necessary.

Now, instead of getting all wordy on you this close to the end of the chapter, let's just handle this by going through the elements in order and discussing how they pertain to the situation above, shall we? To begin, the baseline in this situation has been significantly disrupted by the employee's lie. Now I know this seems wrong considering that car trouble and being sick are common problems, however, getting into a car accident is not a common problem and it also elevates the situation because the potential of personal injury and death is involved. But won't that trigger their surveillance system, you ask? Good point. Sure, this serious nature of the lie is going to activate the receiver's surveillance system but given that the baseline of the receiver is one of a busy organizer who does not have a close personal relationship with the employee, this surveillance state will be short-lived.

Furthermore, the employee is not in the presence of the organizer, so even though their surveillance system has been temporarily activated they are not in a position to probe the employee for deception as this would not only be socially unacceptable to do immediately after an accident, but also because the baseline of a charity organizer would suggest that this particular organizer's personality traits include a lot of empathy and compassion. In other words, their focus is going to be on the safety of their employees, not on the charity's bottom line.

SIDENOTE

Sometimes you have to activate your Subject's surveillance system, but so long as you know that Subject's baseline, you should be able to figure out how to do so tactfully and without a ton of drama. I.e., know what objects trigger them and what story will avoid these cognitive obstacles.

The second and third elements can be looked at together for this situation. This is to say that in this scenario there are three potential lines of verifiability and three potential friction points. These are the employee themself, the tow truck company, and the shop the vehicle is currently in. Now, I'll have you note that the friend who "borrowed" the car is not included in this because the organizer does not have access to them. With that said, though, if the employee needed, they could include a friend in their manipulation to further reinforce that their lie was true. In lay terms, the employee could have their friend vouch for them, thus forcing a curious organizer to believe that, not just one, but two people simply came up with this story, which is not very likely. I mean, what kind of a psycho would go that far out of their way to pull off a lie like this? Well......anyway, I digress.

The tow truck company is easy to handle because you can either say it happened so fast you don't know who the company was, that your friend paid for it, or you can recruit a friend to say that they were the one who actually towed the vehicle with their truck (make sure they don't know the friend), not an official company. When it comes to the vehicle shop, this is also easily handled by either making a fake document on Microsoft Word (very easy to do) or just saying that you are going to take it to a private third-party mechanic, whose documents can be low-quality and/or nonexistent. Yes, this is a pain in the ass and carries with it inherent risk but is also something that will more than likely not be needed in the first place because, if you remember, the baseline of the organizer is that of a kind and empathetic person (Do your baseline analyses beforehand!). Furthermore, and in addition to this, because this is not a profession that requires your vehicle (management), as food delivery for a pizza parlor would, the charity should not necessarily need access to your vehicle repair documents. In fact, the only reason they would ask for this "proof" is if they believe you are lying, and this, again, is unlikely given their baseline and the fact that this is not indicative of a disruptive pattern, which is the fifth element.

SIDENOTE

If you don't feel like you can handle all of those lines of verifiability, you could also just say your car got hit and you barely got it home, or to your friend's house. A friend who is a mechanic by the way. Just food for thought and proof that, as long as you follow the guidelines, you can craft whatever manipulation works best for you and your situation.

Ok, to quickly cover the fourth and fifth elements, as previously discussed, this situation creates such a large disruption from the baseline that, at face value, and considering the baselines of the "good" employee, the environment, and the boss, it is far more likely that the story is true than that the employee just randomly came up with this complicated of a lie. Especially considering that, to cover the fifth element in more depth, this behavior is not part of a disruptive pattern. Of course, if it was, however, indicative of a pattern and you had done this or something similar to it a couple of times this year, well, then you will probably be asked to provide documentation. Furthermore, if this is the case, then the organizer may already be suspicious of you and their initial reaction, when their surveillance system is activated, may not be to care about your health, but rather to wonder if you are lying, again. So, yeah, don't forget that all of these elements work together. I digress though.

At any rate, since this is not a pattern, at least in the situation I presented above, and because this lie meets all of the elemental requirements of a level-three lie, it is very likely that this situation's manipulation will be successful. In fact, during my research, this specific situation received the response "I believe them" over 92% of the time, compared to only 17% with the level-two lie.

SIDENOTE

I feel, after that last paragraph, that I should share how these situations were presented to the participants of my experiment. Basically, after they saw the initial question that you saw about "just trying to be honest," the individuals viewed all of the situations in a randomized order. This is to say that they were not able to simply watch a situations progress in a way that they knew when it was more likely that the person in the scenario was lying. Anyway, as I said earlier, after each situation four answer options were available. "I believe them," "I mostly believe them," "I mostly do not believe them," and "I do not believe them." Now if you are wondering why I included the "mostly" responses, the reason is that these allowed me to measure the data regarding the difference in potency between level-one/level-three lies and level-two/level-four lies more specifically and with more detail.

Alright everyone, that sums up level-three lies, but I want to give you a final warning regarding these lies because people often get addicted to their potency and end up using them more than once (which incidentally zaps their unique power and actually results in them having an adverse effect on manipulation). As I said before, these lies can only be used once. Now it feels repetitive to use the work metaphor again, even though that is what the title of this book references, so instead I will use a new example to elaborate on this topic.

Imagine a situation in which you have made all 7 of the 12 total rent payments in a yearlong lease, on time, but for whatever reason you cannot pay your rent for the month and will be 3 weeks late. Perhaps you owe a gambling debt or got a DUI, shitbag. Regardless of the reason, you have a baseline of paying your rent on time, which works in your favor, but your landlord is not going to believe a level-one or level-two lie, such as your bank is taking a long time or your employer is behind, mainly because they hear these types of lies non-stop. Furthermore, they are a Nazi about rent being on time and will fuck with your lease if you do not calm them down. Oh yeah, and to add to the chaos, your roommate will also be furious because you two are not particularly close and they are very anal about rent being on-time. So what's the plan?

Though this is not an ideal situation by any means, a level-three lie may have the potency to get you out of this jam without a proverbial scratch. Of course, it will rely on you hitting that sweet spot between unbelievable and absurd. Here is a method of ensuring you hit that sweet spot that I used personally.

In the aforementioned situation you could claim that your identity has been stolen. Now, you should not come right out with this revelation because that sounds shady, obviously, but you should do your best to lay the groundwork for it. I.e., over the days leading up to the friction point of your manipulation/deception, start by asking the office janitorial staff and your roommate if they have a missing wallet, credit card, and/or ID in their possession. And if you and your roommate have acquaintances in common, contact them and be aggressive and emotional while asking them to pull the plug on any pranks they may be pulling as well. But just be careful on this second part, though, because even though using emotion would be prudent to demonstrate sincerity, if you use too much then those around you may sense deception or fraud, especially if you are not normally emotional. So, in lay terms, just stay around your emotional baseline, but with a slight disruption. I digress though.

Claiming your identity has been stolen is something that is very rare. However, if you have a history of paying for things adequately and on time then even though this will be a big deal, it will not seem like a cheap excuse, especially if they can think back on how disturbed you have been while looking for your ID and wallet. You see, all of these things you did to lay the groundwork (with level-one lies about a missing wallet, credit cards, and ID) makes this strategy one that should ease the friction point of the manipulation (that you do not have the money) and get you some slack from your landlord and/ or roommate. Of course, again, you obviously cannot use this story more than once, but this one time it would be very hard for another individual to call you out on this deception because, well, who goes to that extreme over their first late rent payment? Put plainly, the chances you simply made this whole thing up randomly is very unlikely due to the complexity of the situation (which is a false reality you created) and your track record.

SIDENOTE

This situation also does a good job of showing us how level-one lies can be very useful when it comes to laying the groundwork for a level-three lie. Case in point, all of those interactions wherein you were searching for your ID and/or wallet were ones that used a level-one lie. Remember that at the beginning of this chapter I called level-one lies menial stories. Well, asking about your wallet is not going to arouse suspicion because it is not obvious what the motive of that lie is. In other words, why would you lie about losing your wallet (assuming they aren't thinking you can't pay rent)?

Furthermore, what the individuals you are telling these level-one lies do not know is that you are altering their associative network models by implanting a node for "missing wallet" right next to the node for yourself. So, when their cognition evaluates your level-three lie about a stolen identity, this node will be fresh in their mind and the connection to you will be strong. Ergo, by using level-one lies to lay the groundwork, you have bolstered your chances of success when it comes to dropping the friction point of your level-three lie. Also, and as a bonus for your landlord, by talking to the janitorial staff you have built a reputable and trustworthy channel through which you can deliver a message that supports your level-three lie. I.e., you can tell your landlord to "Talk to your coworkers. They have seen me looking for my wallet all week." Just food for thought, but let's get to the final level of lying, level-four, which will be short and sweet.

I like to describe level-four lies as "False stories that disrupt the baseline to such an extent that they are obviously a lie and would require that the receiver is reliant on faith in order to be believed." To illustrate, if a level-three lie is, "I got cancer," then a level-four lie is that you were abducted by aliens.

Now, for clarity, these lies typically fall at the end of a spree of lying and are the ugly result of casually throwing out lies until you have woven yourself into an inescapable situation. This downward spiral then forces the sender to either come clean, which humans do not like doing, or to throw out a Hail Mary. And these Hail Mary's very rarely work because instead of allowing the listener to easily believe the lie, they put a disproportional amount of responsibility on the listener to think centrally about what they are hearing, which as it turns out, for a level-four lie is going to be an extremely unlikely scenario. In lay terms, these lies are level-two lies on steroids and require an extensive amount of proof and/or evidence to be believed.

Truth be told, I do not feel the need to spend a lot of time on these lies because, if I am being honest, level-four lies are largely irrelevant. The reason, as I said earlier, most lies will be "bad" lies, which means that they could potentially work, but likely will not. Well, level-four lies are the fringe sector of these "bad" lies and you honestly will not see them very often. Plus, if you do and someone around you is using these, they will be easy to spot. Good to go?

Now, just something to consider here at the outset of this section, if you yourself are at a place where you feel a level-four lie is necessary, I would advise you to stop, zoom out to 30,000 feet, look down at your situation, and then assess why you are in this position. Why, you ask? Well, the chances that escalating your already failing deception will work are slim to none, so maybe it would be better to instead readjust and find a new way. Anyway, like I said, I want this part to be short and sweet because this level of lie is both not common and not difficult to classify. But with that said, I will still include the elements of a level-four lie, as well as two examples of a level-four lie, below this paragraph. Take a look at them, analyze them, and see if you can break down the individual elements on your own, which at this point, I hope you can. (Hint: The main difference between a level-two and a level-four lie involves the level of baseline disruption.)

Level 4

1) The lie creates a significant disruption from the baseline.

2) The lie can contain a direct line or multiple lines of verifiability; however, one or more of these are not substantive (proof/witness testimony/documentation), and therefore are a liability (I.e., you lie and say you got your friend's car *your boss knows the friend and the friend will not back up your story* in a wreck and had it towed to a repair shop *your bosses brother owns the repair shop and will not verify your story*.)

3) The lie can have one source of friction or many.

4) The lie is so absurd that it is unreasonable to assume, barring noteworthy evidence, that the teller is speaking the truth.

5) The lie can be representative of a disruptive pattern.

Situation 1:

A mid-level manager at a new tech start-up receives a call from an entry-level employee 45 minutes before their shift stating that they will not be able to make it to work. Their explanation was that they were in a terrible accident. They flipped their car, totaling it, and their roommate and brother, who were also in the car, had to go to the hospital. They also have the flu and are throwing up. They say that they will be back in a day or two. They also mention that they can't get the receipts from the shop because the shop's printer is down.

Situation 2:

A spouse finds a bill for a divorce attorney in their garbage. The name on the bill is their marital partners' name, and the reason line states, "initial consult." The spouse checks the bank records and finds no record of the event. After some investigation, they discover that their significant other has been funneling small amounts of money into a secret account. The spouse has noticed a distance in the relationship for a while, but the couple has been together for 4 years, so this could be a normal lull. The spouse confronts their significant other. That significant other says that they didn't meet with the lawyer and that actually it was a friend, whom the spouse knows, who didn't want their partner of 5 years to find out. They go on to say that this is why it is under the spouse's partner's name. The

partner tells the spouse that the friend's partner is secretly abusive and not the person they both thought, something that shocks the spouse. The partner also says that the bank account is a secret fund they have been saving up so that they can take the spouse on a surprise vacation, and that the friend was planning to pay the money back for the attorney consult, and not to worry about it.

Spoiler alert, in both of these situations there is a massive baseline disruption, many ways for the receiver to verify the sender is lying, and multiple friction points. Ergo, without serious evidence backing up their claims, which they do not have because all of these situations are lies, it is not very likely that the people in these scenarios will be believed. Now, in regard to being representative of a disruptive pattern, this is why I say bad lies *can* be representative of a pattern. I.e., in the first scenario, there is no pattern included. However, in the second scenario there is (the growing distance). Capeesh? Sweet, then in that case, see you all in the next and final chapter wherein we will be talking about how to put all of this together.

What is the System

The mind is a superb instrument if used rightly. Used wrongly, however, it becomes very destructive. To put it more accurately, it is not so much that you use your mind wrongly – you usually don't use it at all. It uses you. This is the disease. You believe that you are your mind. This is the delusion. The instrument has taken you over. —**Eckhart Tolle**

Well friends, it appears we have reached the final chapter and also the end of this book. I have to say that this was a very enjoyable journey and, to my surprise, has also been one that has significantly improved my own understanding of the principles, concepts, and theories surrounding the topic of manipulation. To that end, I suppose it's true that when you have to teach something you end up becoming even more well-versed in it, and that I should thank all of you for giving me that opportunity. This is to say that, even though I do not know you personally and may never speak to you in person, over the phone, or through email, all of you reading and/or listening to this are still the primary reason I decided to combine all of this research and put it into book form. So, thank you.

Now, for those who are faint of heart, I recognize that, for better or worse, I have a very blunt view of human nature and the communication process that comes with it, and after that first chapter this is a view that you are no doubt familiar with. Regardless of this somewhat grim view of humanity, though, it is important to me that you know I still want the best for humanity. In other words, much like I want every citizen to engage in firearms training, basic medical training, and tactical home defense training, I also want a well-armed population when it comes to the communication process, which, as I have said many times throughout this book, is simply a form of manipulation. Sure, this may have cast this book, and my research as a whole with a rather dark overtone, ethically speaking that is, and it may even make me seem like a pessimist and/or a person suffering from paranoia; nonetheless, my objective in this book, as warped as it may seem to a normal vanilla westerner, was to do something good for humanity. So, with that said, I want to sincerely say thank you to the more faint-hearted folks as well for reading and/or listening. Ok, now that I got that out of the way it is time to give you the final piece of my framework for manipulation, deception, and misdirection.

So, what is this system of manipulation that I have been alluding to for the last seven chapters? Well, and don't hate me for this, you have actually already seen/learned the system, albeit in small segments, and have it all in your mind right now at this very moment. You see, my work started off with the hypothesis that there are four dimensions of lying and that somehow it is possible to use this information to manipulate the perceived reality of others. And I proved this to be true, however, the journey to get there led me down a path that allowed the four dimensions of lying and the six archetypes of power to bring it all together. Now, as I have said numerous times throughout this book, there is no one size fits all solution when it comes to manipulation. I mean, sure, there are well established theories and concepts with rules and tenants, and furthermore there is a very specific dimensional landscape of the four types of lies; but even with this information, every subject, sender, message, channel, receiver, and social environment, along with its baseline, will be different.

Because of this, it would be dishonest of me to try and formulate/pass on some hacky checklist wherein you have to say or do something specific that will work for every scenario. No, that may look good on paper and sell more books, but it would simply not allow you, the reader and/or listener enough longitude and latitude to manipulate efficiently in your specific environment. You see, the way I look at it is this. If I was a mechanic and I taught you how to work on several different types of cars, yes, you would be able to fix these cars quickly and effectively when they came into your shop, but you would still be limited in your overall knowledge of automobiles. If instead of this, however, I was to teach you all of the principles behind combustion engines, transmissions, and modern cooling systems, well, it may take more time and thought on your end, but you would also be able to work on pretty much any automobile that came your way. The latter is what this book is designed to be, but in terms of manipulation, not automobiles.

Now, even though I just said that you already know the system, now that you have an understanding of what perceived reality is, how to form a baseline, all of the individual elements of manipulation/persuasion, and how our cognition uses these elements, I still want to give you a few reminders of how all of these concepts work together to form my framework. The reason, if nothing else, this will reiterate the most important parts of this book for manipulators, and, I suppose, also those who want a better understanding of this process so that they can spot when they are being manipulated and when they should see those around them as a threat. Sound good? Great.

First off, what is real does not always matter during the manipulation process. Instead, what *may* be real, at least to your Subject, is often of much greater importance. This is because people technically operate based upon their perceptions of reality, not objective reality. Therefore, you as the manipulator have a great deal of opportunity when it comes to molding your Subject's reality. Maybe this is a reality in which you have to work 60 hours a week instead of 40, which gives you 20 hours of free time to do something else. Or perhaps it is a reality wherein you have a medical condition and need to have the ability to control your own hours. Whatever your specific situation is, you can use the tools in this book to make the reality others exist in one that is conducive to your own personal goals.

Second, it is crucial, not just for manipulation, but also for maintaining control over your life, that you learn to and also practice establishing baselines. This includes baselines of your environment, of course, but also baselines of the individuals within that environment. You see, humans are often unpredictable and irrational and this can make their behavior difficult to understand/predict, but with a thorough understanding of their baseline this becomes much easier. To that end, as you already know when it comes to forming a manipulation strategy that uses the proper ELM route, the proper SMCR structure, and also one that avoids any manipulative potholes that will engage your Subject's surveillance system, hot cognition, and/or motivated reasoning, baselines give you an incredible amount of reliable and actionable data. So, when it comes to planning a manipulation strategy, or even just having the option available to you if you should decide to put one into motion, pay attention to everything. Furthermore, pay attention to not only your environment itself, but also what causes things to alter the environment you are in and/or the behavior of those within it. Case in point, if you want to manipulate your band so that you can change its name, are the members more agreeable before or after a show? Are they more likely to follow one specific member whom you can approach solo, or are they more open to new ideas when they are all together? You should be cataloging all of these things, and many more like them, and then storing all of that information for future use.

Third, while you are forming your baselines of the people around you, do not forget to take note of how their cognition works. I.e., are they deliberate thinkers who are more likely to use their LTM, or are they busy bodies that are always overthinking everything and using their on-line/working memory? Do they use heuristics a lot? If so, what type of heuristics do they use most often and how difficult are these to change? And in addition to these considerations, what topics drive them to use motivated reasoning, and when they use motivated reasoning is it honest or in bad faith; and also, can this be leveraged to give them the illusion of power over you or to misdirect their attention to something irrelevant while you attempt to change their attitude about something else entirely? And last but not least, is the individual an emotional person, or a more even keeled type of person? You should know this before starting your manipulation because, as we already know, hot cognition is not limited to negative emotions like anger or fear and can make a Subject highly irrational and/or unpredictable. Ergo, all of these things you should take into consideration because these cognitive factors, or, more specifically, how your Subject's mind works individually can give you more detailed insights into what style of manipulation you should use.

The fourth thing to remember is that, building upon all of the other elements of the manipulation process, you can and should use the academic models of persuasion to form an actionable strategy. Now, even though many academics would say that you should stick to just one model, I am and have always been a fan of hybrid models, and this applies to pretty much everything involving human behavior because, in my experience, human behavior is much too complex to box in. With that in mind, unlike those other academics I would suggest using the individual SMCR elements of the persuasion process, along with the ELM, to form a unique strategy for your Subject. In other words, when planning to manipulate an individual first take into consideration how much elaboration the Subject is likely to use when it comes to the friction point of your manipulation (understanding their baseline/cognitive norms should help with this step). Then, when this analysis is complete, this will give you a good starting point from which you can assess what form the individual elements of your manipulation should take. I.e., perhaps your Subject will use the peripheral route, and therefore, the channel and sender are the most important parts of the puzzle because, if they are correctly structured, the Subject of your manipulation will not look very close at the message itself. Conversely, though, maybe the Subject will use the central route and you should instead use misdirection to focus them on the merits of the actual message and *not* who is saying it. Regardless of how your particular situation looks, if you have used your baseline analysis skills to understand your Subject's normal cognitive processing style, you should be able to use this information, and the information contained within the fifth chapter to structure a manipulation strategy that is perfectly tailored to fit your Subject's individual quirks and/or personality traits.

Ok, almost there folks so stay with me. The fifth thing to remember is that actualized power and/or position is not, in and of itself, a good metric to use for measuring societal worth. I bring this up because during my research I often overlooked those with low levels of actual worth and found, more often than one would think, that this led to an inaccurate baseline analysis. Inevitably, this also disrupted the follow-on parts of my manipulation strategies and I had to experience the distasteful and humiliating sting of failure in these situations. So, avoid this problem and simply approach each baseline analysis with a clean slate and no preconceived notions about the Subject.

The sixth thing to remember, which is also kind of related to the fifth if I am being honest, is that not everyone handles power the same. To that end, according to my research there are six basic archetypes that you can use to help yourself understand the different ways that people handle power. This information, though not necessarily a collection of hard and fast rules, can be invaluable when establishing baselines and understanding your Subject's cognitive processing style. Furthermore, it can be extremely beneficial for manipulators because, after you have formed a manipulation strategy using all of the other concepts and theories in this book, you can know what things in your environment might change when the Subject receives power. These changes, as previously mentioned in this book, are something you will experience regularly because people are, after all, most easily manipulated when they feel that they are in a position of power over you, and therefore, your strategy should, if it follows my framework, seek to give them this illusion of power.

Alright, the seventh and final thing I want you to remember is that even though most manipulations will involve some form of deception, not all deceptions are created equal. This is to say that some will be "good" deceptions and some will be "bad" deceptions. To clarify this a bit, good deceptions will be more likely to be believed than bad deceptions, despite the fact that bad deceptions make up the lion's share of the deceptions we see on a regular basis. If you are planning on using deception in your manipulation strategy, utilize the four-dimensional classification system I outlined in the seventh chapter of this book to double-check that your chosen deceptions are either a level-one or level-three lie. The reason for this is that it is very easy to tell a bad lie (level-two and level-four lies), but if you can form a lie that meets all of the requirements of a level-one or level-three lie you will, statistically, have much more success. Just do not forget that, though very potent, a level-three lie can only be used once. Furthermore, you should also not forget that no lie has a 100% success rate. So, if your situation permits this strategy, use level-one lies to lay the groundwork for your level-three lie as this can only raise your chances of success. Case in point, if you remember the example I gave about the person who could not pay rent then you also remember that I explained how the individual used level-one lies to make everyone believe that they had, in fact, lost their wallet; and that this made the friction point of telling the landlord and roommate that their identity had been stolen go much smoother.

Well, I suppose that is it. I truly cannot believe we are here, but I really don't have anything else to add. In closing, I hope that you enjoyed taking this ride with me and I sincerely hope this work helps you in your day to day life. You see, we are in the middle of a giant evolutionarily driven competition fueled and sponsored by human nature, and because of this many people often find themselves on the losing side of this competition, which sucks. If for no other reason than you took the time to read and/or listen to my book, I do not want that for you. Rather, I see you as a part of my in-group now and want you to be someone who is an active participant in their own life, and not someone who is a slave to the goals and objectives of others.

Anyway, with that said, go forth and use my research to do great things for yourself, whether that means rising to the top of your corporate ladder, restoring balance to the power structures of your personal relationships, or even just getting a much needed day off by figuring out How To Get Out Of Work.

References....
for the Nerds

Adoree Durayappah-Harrison. *9 Truths You Should Know About Expert Liars | Psychology Today*. (n.d.). Www.psychologytoday.com. https://www.psychologytoday.com/us/blog/thriving101/202002/9-truths-you-should- know-about-expert-liars

Ajzen, I. (1985). From intentions to actions: A theory of planned behavior. In J. Kuhl & J. Beckmann (Eds.), *Action control: From cognition to behavior. Berlin,* Heidelber, New York: Springer-Verlag. (pp. 11-39).

Ajzen, I. (2005). *Attitudes, Personality and Behaviour* . New York: Open University press.

Alford, J. R., & Hibbing, J. R. (2004). The Origin of Politics: An Evolutionary Theory of Political Behavior. *Perspectives on Politics,* 2(4), 707–723. http://www.jstor.org/stable/3688539

Anderson, A., & Smith, L. (2013). Dynamic Deception. American Economic Review, 103(7), 2811–2847. https://doi.org/10.1257/aer.103.7.2811

Anthony Harris. (2020, August 5). *10 Different Types of Lies People Tell Others*. The Scope. https://kiwisearches.com/blog/different-types-of-lies-people-tell-others/

Aronson, E., & Mills, J. (1959). The effect of severity of initiation on liking for a group. *The Journal of Abnormal and Social Psychology,* 59(2), 177-181.

Batson, C. D. (2018). The Pleasure of Empathic Joy. In *Oxford Scholarship Online*. Oxford University Press. https://doi.org/10.1093/oso/9780190651374.003.0008

Batson, C. D., Batson, J. G., Slingsby, J. K., Harrell, K. L., Peekna, H. M., & Todd, R. M. (1991). Empathic joy and the empathy-altruism hypothesis. *Journal of Personality and Social Psychology, 61*(3), 413–426. https://doi.org/10.1037/0022-3514.61.3.413

Bartels, L. M. (2002). Beyond the Running Tally: Partisan Bias in Political Perceptions. *Political Behavior, 24*(2), 117–150. https://doi.org/10.1023/a:1021226224601

Baumeister, R.F. (1982). A self-presentational view of social phenomena. *Psychological Bulletin, 91*, 3-26.

Beaman, A. L., Klentz, B., Diener, E., & Svanum, S. (1979). Self-awareness and transgression in children: Two field studies. *Journal of Personality and Social Psychology, 37* (10), 1835–1846.

Bem, D. J. (1972). Self-perception theory. In L. Berkowitz (Ed.), *Advances in experimental social psychology* (Vol. 6, pp. 1-62). New York: Academic Press.

Bester, H., & Güth, W. (1998). Is altruism evolutionarily stable? *Journal of Economic Behavior & Organization, 34*(2), 193–209. https://doi.org/10.1016/s0167-2681(97)00060-7

Bhatt, M. A., Lohrenz, T., Camerer, C. F., & Montague, P. R. (2010). Neural signatures of strategic types in a two-person bargaining game. *Proceedings of the National Academy of Sciences, 107*(46), 19720–19725. https://doi.org/10.1073/pnas.1009625107

Brehm, J. W. (1956). Postdecision changes in the desirability of alternatives. *The Journal of Abnormal and Social Psychology, 52*(3), 384-389.

Buscemi, J. (2020, February 20). *How to Be a Better Liar*. Forge. https://forge.medium.com/how-to-be-a-better-liar-b023e9b8da23

Camacho, G., Reinka, M. A., & Quinn, D. M. (2020). Disclosure and concealment of stigmatized identities. *Current Opinion in Psychology, 31*, 28–32. https://doi.org/10.1016/j.copsyc.2019.07.031

Cialdini, R. B. (1985). *Influence: how and why people agree to things*. Quill.

Cialdini, R. B. (2007). *Influence: The Psychology of Persuasion*. Collins. (Original work published 1984)

Cialdini, R. B. (2014). *Influence: science and practice* (5th ed.). Pearson Education.

Cialdini, R. B. (2016). *Pre-suasion: a revolutionary way to influence and persuade*. Simon & Schuster Paperbacks.

Chisholm, R. M., & Feehan, T. D. (1977). The Intent to Deceive. *The Journal of Philosophy, 74*(3), 143–159. JSTOR. https://doi.org/10.2307/2025605

Choshen-Hillel, S., Shaw, A., & Caruso, E. M. (2020). Lying to appear honest. *Journal of Experimental Psychology: General, 149*(9), 1719–1735. https://doi.org/10.1037/xge0000737

Church, K. (2018, June 4). *The three types of lies*. Medium. https://kchurch05.medium.com/the- three-types-of-lies-d4c014296e72

Ettinger, D., & Jehiel, P. (2010). A Theory of Deception. *American Economic Journal: Microeconomics, 2*(1), 1–20. https://doi.org/10.1257/mic.2.1.1

Faulkner, P. (2007). What Is Wrong with Lying? *Philosophy and Phenomenological Research, 75*(3), 535–557. https://doi.org/10.1111/j.1933-1592.2007.00092.x

Fallis, D. (2009). What Is Lying? *The Journal of Philosophy, 106*(1), 29–56. http://www.jstor.org/stable/20620149

Fallis, D. (2014). Skyrms on the possibility of universal deception. *Philosophical Studies, 172*(2), 375–397. https://doi.org/10.1007/s11098-014-0308-x

Festinger, L. (1957). *A theory of cognitive dissonance*. Stanford, Calif.: Stanford University Press.

Festinger, L., & Carlsmith, J. M. (1959). Cognitive consequences of forced compliance. *The Journal of Abnormal and Social Psychology, 58*(2), 203–210.

Freedman, J. L., & Fraser, S. C. (1966). Compliance without pressure: The foot-in-the-door technique. *Journal of Personality and Social Psychology, 4* (2), 195–202.

Fulmer, I. S., Barry, B., & Long, D. A. (2008). Lying and Smiling: Informational and Emotional Deception in Negotiation. *Journal of Business Ethics, 88*(4), 691–709. https://doi.org/10.1007/s10551-008-9975-x

Green, D. P., & Gerber, A. S. (2019). *Get out the vote : how to increase voter turnout.* Brookings Institution Press.

Greenwashing and the 3 Types of Lies | EM SC 470: Applied Sustainability in Contemporary Culture. (n.d.). Www.e-Education.psu.edu. Retrieved December 26, 2022, from https://www.e-education.psu.edu/emsc470/node/67

Haney, C., Banks, W. C., & Zimbardo, P. G. (1973). Study of prisoners and guards in a simulated prison. *Naval Research Reviews, 9* (1-17). Washington, DC: Office of Naval Research.

Ibitz, S. (2022, August 24). *3 Types of Lies and How to Find Out.* Human Behavior Lab. https://humanbehaviorlab.com/3-types-of-lies-and-how-to-find-out/

Inc, G. (2004, December 7). *Smoking.* Gallup.com. https://news.gallup.com/poll/14257/smoking.aspx

James, E. (2019). Nonhuman Fictional Characters and the Empathy-Altruism Hypothesis. *Poetics Today, 40*(3), 579–596. https://doi.org/10.1215/03335372-7558164

Jeff Wise. *Top Ten Secrets of Effective Liars | Psychology Today.* (n.d.). Www.psychologytoday.com. Retrieved December 26, 2022, from https://www.psychologytoday.com/intl/blog/extreme-fear/201005/top-ten-secrets- effective-liars

Kashy, D. A., & DePaulo, B. M. (1996). Who lies? *Journal of Personality and Social Psychology, 70*(5), 1037–1051. https://doi.org/10.1037/0022-3514.70.5.1037

Kawamichi, H., Tanabe, H. C., Takahashi, H. K., & Sadato, N. (2013). Activation of the reward system during sympathetic concern is mediated by two types of empathy in a familiarity- dependent manner. *Social Neuroscience, 8*(1), 90–100. https://doi.org/10.1080/17470919.2012.744349

Kenrick, D. T., Goldstein, N. J., & Braver, S. L. (2012). *Six degrees of social influence : science, application, and the psychology of Robert Cialdini.* Oxford University Press.

Le Bot, J.-M. (2014). A Clinical Perspective on "Theory of Mind", Empathy and Altruism: the Hypothesis of Somasia. *Relations, 2.1,* 91–107. https://doi.org/10.7358/rela-2014-001- lebo

MacKuen, M. B., Erikson, R. S., & Stimson, J. A. (1989). Macropartisanship. *The American Political Science Review, 83*(4), 1125–1142. https://doi.org/10.2307/1961661

Mares, A. C., & Turvey, B. E. (2018). The Psychology of Lying. *False Allegations,* 21–36. https://doi.org/10.1016/b978-0-12-801250-5.00002-1

McGrath, M., & Turvey, B. E. (2018). False Allegations and Malingering. *False Allegations,* 37– 63. https://doi.org/10.1016/b978-0-12-801250-5.00003-3

Nax, H. H., & Rigos, A. (2015). Assortativity Evolving from Social Dilemmas. *SSRN Electronic Journal.* https://doi.org/10.2139/ssrn.2664638

Newton, J. (2017). Shared intentions: The evolution of collaboration. *Games and Economic Behavior, 104,* 517–534. https://doi.org/10.1016/j.geb.2017.06.001

Paine, S. C. (1989). Persuasion, Manipulation, and Dimension. *The Journal of Politics, 51*(1), 36–49. https://doi.org/10.2307/2131608

Perry, D., Hendler, T., & Shamay-Tsoory, S. G. (2011). Can we share the joy of others? Empathic neural responses to distress vs joy. *Social Cognitive and Affective Neuroscience, 7*(8), 909–916. https://doi.org/10.1093/scan/nsr073

Pittinsky, T. L., & Montoya, R. M. (2016). Empathic Joy in Positive Intergroup Relations. *Journal of Social Issues, 72*(3), 511–523. https://doi.org/10.1111/josi.12179

Randall J. Boyle, Jeffrey A. Clements, & Jeffrey Gainer Proudfoot. (2018). Measuring Deception: A Look at Antecedents to Deceptive Intent. *The American Journal of Psychology, 131*(3), 347–367. https://doi.org/10.5406/amerjpsyc.131.3.0347

Rasmus Kleis Nielsen. (2012). *Ground wars: personalized communication in political campaigns.* Princeton University Press.

Repke, M. A., Conway, L. G., & Houck, S. C. (2017). The Strategic Manipulation of Linguistic Complexity: A Test of Two Models of Lying. *Journal of Language and Social Psychology, 37*(1), 74–92. https://doi.org/10.1177/0261927x17706943

Rose, T. (2022). *Collective illusions: conformity, complicity, and the science of why we make bad decisions.* Hachette Books.

Ryan, C., & Cacilda Jethá. (2011). *Sex at dawn: how we mate, why we stray, and what it means for modern relationships.* Harper.

Schroeder, D. A., Graziano, W. G., Batson, C. D., Lishner, D. A., & Stocks, E. L. (2015). The Empathy–Altruism Hypothesis. *The Oxford Handbook of Prosocial Behavior.* https://doi.org/10.1093/oxfordhb/9780195399813.013.023

Seigel, J. (2021, May 19). *The Truth about Lying.* JSTOR Daily. https://daily.jstor.org/the-truth- about-lying/

Shabbir, H., & Thwaites, D. (2007). The Use of Humor to Mask Deceptive Advertising: It's No Laughing Matter. Journal of Advertising, 36(2), 75–85. https://doi.org/10.2753/joa0091- 3367360205

Sheppard, J. A. (2012). The Roots of Deception. *American Intelligence Journal, 30*(2), 17–21. http://www.jstor.org/stable/26202009

Sheeran, P. (2002). Intention—behavior relations: A conceptual and empirical review, *European Review of Social Psychology, 12*(1), 1-36.

Stein, M. (2018). Lying. *Agni, 87,* 70–83. http://www.jstor.org/stable/44984134

Stocks, E. L., Lishner, D. A., & Decker, S. K. (2008). Altruism or psychological escape: Why does empathy promote prosocial behavior? *European Journal of Social Psychology, 39*(5), 649–665. https://doi.org/10.1002/ejsp.561

The 15 types of lies (and their characteristics) | [2022]. (2021, June 15). https://enorcerna.com/wiki/psychology/the-15-types-of-lies-and-their-characteristics

Van Dijk, T. A. (2006). Discourse and manipulation. *Discourse & Society*, *17*(3), 359–383. https://doi.org/10.1177/0957926506060250

Verigin, B. L., Meijer, E. H., Bogaard, G., & Vrij, A. (2019). Lie prevalence, lie characteristics and strategies of self-reported good liars. *PLOS ONE*, *14*(12), e0225566. https://doi.org/10.1371/journal.pone.0225566

Verschuere, B., Spruyt, A., Meijer, E. H., & Otgaar, H. (2011). The ease of lying. *Consciousness and Cognition*, *20*(3), 908–911. https://doi.org/10.1016/j.concog.2010.10.023

Walton, A. G. (n.d.). *New Study Finds People May Actually Lie To Appear More Honest*. Forbes. Retrieved December 26, 2022, from https://www.forbes.com/sites/alicegwalton/2020/01/31/do-you-lie-to-appear-honest-new- study-looks-at-the-phenomenon

Wicker, A. W. (1969). Attitudes versus actions: The relationship of verbal and overt behavioral responses to attitude objects. *Journal of Social Issues*, *25* (4), 41–78.

Williams, E. J., Bott, L. A., Patrick, J., & Lewis, M. B. (2013). Telling Lies: The Irrepressible Truth? *PLoS ONE*, *8*(4), e60713. https://doi.org/10.1371/journal.pone.0060713

About the Author

Alexander Oakes is a Marine Corps combat veteran with a BA in Political Science and an MA in Political Psychology. He is currently pursuing his PhD in Clinical Psychology at Arizona State University while he writes for The Mises Institute, Human Events, and The Thinking Conservative. He is also beginning to produce video content on all social media platforms (X, YouTube, Spotify, Rumble, etc.) under the handle @authoralexoakes.